'Maggie Hamilton guides us, with an expert's touch, into the rich and remarkably complex world of fairies. Her own stories, and those of many others who have come forward to share their experiences of these tiny beings, makes for fascinating reading. As if I was being guided through a beautiful meditation, the book opened my eyes and heart to the other lives that are all around us if only we take the time to look. Once you've read *Inside the Life of Fairies,* you'll never see the world in quite the same way again!'
—Candida Baker MA, President Equus Alliance, Australia

'This beautifully written book took my right back to the halcyon days of my childhood in the beautiful Yorkshire Dales, when summer was endless, and time stood still. Maggie reawakens the magic and wonder of nature and transported me through true stories of people who see through the mists of reality, into those time-honoured spaces where fairies and the little people truly exist in their own world, creating harmony and magic. She has awakened the part of me that once again appreciates the wonder of natural spaces, where the fairies work so hard to nurture, the scent of the blossom so carefully tended by them, and the sweet song of the blackbird as I walk through the woods and touch the warm, soft bark of the trees, and my heart bursts with love. This is an incredibly uplifting book, for both young and old, reminding us that wherever we may be, the fairies are always amongst us bringing their sparkles and luminous experiences just waiting to touch our hearts and minds.'
—Heather Hoyland, spiritual medium, Yorkshire, England

'This enchanting book took me on a wonderful journey into the life of fairies. I must say that since reading it, not a day has gone by without me having a new, inspiring thought about it. I love trees so 'The Miracle of Trees' chapter certainly made me think quite differently about the trees around me and their tiny inhabitants. I often pick up pebbles and stones just to 'feel' them, so to read 'rocks and stones sit silently among us, preciously guarding their memories of people and events long gone' really resonated with me. A truly magical and compelling read.'
—Wendy Nute, Halwyn Holistics, Snell's Beach, New Zealand.

'If your mind is open to explore the world of Faeries this book offers many aspects of the unknown. Possibly opening your mind and heart to past unexplained encounters and put you on the path to invite the Faeries into your future life.'
—Lynda Collier, Collier's Crystals and Gifts,
Blue Mountains, Australia

Inside the Secret Life of Fairies

Where Dreams Come True

Maggie Hamilton

HAY HOUSE, INC.
Carlsbad, California • New York City
London • Sydney • New Delhi

Published in Australia by: Hay House Australia Pty. Ltd.: www.hayhouse.com.au
Published in the United States by: Hay House, Inc.: www.hayhouse.com
Published in the United Kingdom by: Hay House UK, Ltd.: www.hayhouse.co.uk
Published in India by: Hay House Publishers India: www.hayhouse.co.in

Design by Rhett Nacson
Typeset by Bookhouse, Sydney
Edited by Margie Tubbs

ISBN: 9781401958886

22 21 20 19   4 3 2 1
1st Australian edition, September 2019

Printed in Australia by McPherson's Printing Group

For Rose

Fairies are wise, enchanting, rather mysterious folk.
When you invite them into your life,
there's no end to the beauty and goodness they will bring.

Contents

Introduction

My very first memory ever was walking in the meadows close to my childhood home with my Scottish grandmother, Rose. It was a perfect summer afternoon. I can still remember the brilliant sunlight, the intense green of the grass. Savouring the gentle warmth of the day, the afternoon slipped away as we talked and laughed, picked buttercups and made daisy chains.

When it came time to leave, we returned to the wooden steps we'd clambered over into the meadow, only to find they were gone. They'd literally vanished! Mystified, I stared up at my grandmother. She smiled and told me there was nothing to worry about, that the fairies were playing tricks on us. All we needed to do was wait for the steps to reappear, she assured me. Within moments, the stairs did reappear and home we went.

This strange incident was soon forgotten. But now as I look back to that golden afternoon, I realise some part of me was claimed by the fairies that day. This fleeting glimpse of the 'other' expanded the way I viewed the world. It captured my imagination, inspiring me to seek out life's enchanted places wherever I found myself. That brief moment in time was an immense gift. It's helped me through life's ups and downs, and has given me much more besides.

Looking back, mine was a simple childhood. There was an innocence to life back then. People had a stronger connection with nature. Though we had fewer possessions, we never felt any sense of lack because nature fed us, body and soul. After the ravages of two world wars, there was a great hunger to embrace the moment. Everyone longed for life to be normal again.

As a family, we walked wherever we needed to go. That's what people did. So my early years were spent wandering in forests and fields, or meandering down English country lanes. This gentle pace meant there was time to take in the world around me. To savour the shifting clouds of bluebells that brought the woods to life in spring. To lose myself in the mysterious patterns etched on the windowpane at the first sign of frost.

When I was five, we went to live in town. Like most children growing up in towns and cities in the fifties, I'd spend weekends and holidays visiting aunts and uncles in the country. So I was drawn into the ancient cycle of seasons. Back then, many more people delighted in seeing the first green shoots nudge their way through the frozen earth. They enjoyed collecting wild berries that flourished by the roadside and wading through the rich carpet of autumn leaves. Simple pleasures warmed and inspired us, as did the many tales shared around the fire once night closed in.

Yet while there were countless opportunities to lose ourselves in the beauty of nature, life was changing. The deep connection people had enjoyed with the land for countless generations was fading. Glimpses of our enchanting fairy friends were becoming less frequent. I see now how fortunate I was to be surrounded by people who often talked of fairy folk. Not as figments of an overactive imagination, but as living presences around us, as caretakers of the natural world.

Those old souls spoke freely of their fairy encounters, which continued to astonish and mesmerise them long after the event. Seeing fairies altered the way they saw things. The way they related to the world around them. The way they walked on the earth and harvested her resources. They felt blessed to have touched the mystical heart of creation.

All too soon my childhood was over. After school and university I travelled, then settled into work, living minutes from the city centre. Life was exhilarating. I gave little thought to the rich gifts of my childhood, until the pain of my forgetfulness became too great. My success did not nourish me. It left my soul hungry, aching for more.

As I began searching for ways to inject more meaning into my day, I began to contemplate our timeless connections with the land. In so doing, I came full circle. I realised that to thrive I needed to explore the intricate world of fairies and all that it teaches about creation. I ached to know more of the astonishing web of life we're all part of. How to walk lightly and wisely on the earth. How to hold a bigger vision for myself and the world. I found myself walking once more in woods, bushland and meadows. Spending time in deserts and by the ocean. As I did so, those parts of me that were sad and out off sorts slowly began to heal.

At one stage I was fortunate to have several weeks alone in the mountains, finishing off a book I was working on. Those weeks were life-changing. As I walked in sun, rain and swirling mists, and experienced the raw force of summer storms, nature began to reveal itself to me in ways I'd never experienced before. I returned to the city changed inside and out.

Back home, I continued to commute and work long hours. Yet exciting as my city life was, it no longer fulfilled me. Every now and then a familiar ache would arise and, heeding the call, I'd immerse myself in nature and be inspired and renewed. This has become a healing pattern for me—taking regular breaks from the crush of city life, then returning home transformed. Sometimes the transformations are subtle, sometimes they shake me up. What I've learnt is that nature never fails me.

Whenever I take time out I'm amazed by how quickly the soul cramp of city life dissolves, as nature's wisdom and loveliness claims me once more. Then when I'm done I gather up all I've learnt and carry it deep in my heart back to the city, determined to create more beauty and solace there. I know now that we can live in big cities and still be plugged into nature. When we acknowledge this, a more profound connection to nature is made available to us in the city. We just have to know where to recognise those places that hold healing and inspiration for us amid the traffic, the crush of buildings and the crowds of people. When we know that the fairy kingdom is available to us everywhere, we're able to create healing spaces for ourselves and others in the most unlikely locations.

The deeper I ventured into the world of fairies, the more I began to meet people from all walks of life who had encountered these otherwordly beings. I was delighted and astonished to talk about fairies to those who worked in corporations or were fresh out of university, just as I did with busy mums and grandmothers, scientists and health practitioners. Some people I met were from very different cultural backgrounds, yet their experiences with fairies were surprisingly similar. Sadly, few had ever spoken of their fairy encounters, because they feared ridicule. Their relief at finally being able to share their precious encounters often moved me to tears.

After years of gathering fairy experiences and reflecting on them, it's time for me to share as much as I can. Have you noticed how something profound happens when we relate stories that matter deeply to us? Such moments can bring healing and delight. They also help us to be more authentic, more in tune with the deeper rhythms of life. While some may dismiss the fairy accounts I share here as absurd, the people I spoke with weren't in the least bit flaky or fanciful. Almost all of them lived and worked in the mainstream. Their encounters with fairies were nearly always unexpected. None of them regretted their brush with our other-worldly friends. For many, such encounters were life-changing. They spoke of the sheer magic of life they now experienced, of their profound reverence for nature.

Like all the best journeys, my journey with the fairies continues. There are many more insights yet to be revealed. Discovering the fullness and beauty of the fairy kingdom takes time and patience. Fairies can be immensely generous, but they do not yield their secrets easily. You have to prove yourself worthy of their trust.

I began this book well over a decade ago, only to have the pieces of this remarkable jigsaw revealed to me little by little. Looking back, I wouldn't have it any other way, because I needed to ponder each precious insight I was given—to appreciate and understand it before I was shown the next possibility and the next.

This process has left me with a much greater passion for life and for living, for seeking out the presence of the divine wherever I am. It's also opened up my perceptions way beyond anything I thought possible. My wish for you is all this and more. I pray that the strangely beautiful, often mysterious ways of the fairies will touch some forgotten part of you, allowing you to feel more alive, more inspired, more whole.

Echoes of Past Enchantments

It's hard to put into words why fairies enchant us so. Fairies are like that. They're mesmerising and mysterious and hard to pin down. At least, that's what fairy stories suggest. But do fairies really exist? And if so, where do fairies live? When and how can we see them? What, if anything, do they demand of us? And what do they think of humankind?

It isn't just fairies who mystify us. So do the many tales of fairy encounters we have in our keeping. Where do these stories come from? How did these spellbinding tales take shape? Were the accounts we have of fairies first born in the flames of a fire on a cold winter's night, or in snatches of dreams scarcely remembered on waking? Or is it possible that these magical tales are remnants of the special relationship we once shared with these strange other-worldly creatures?

Most of us want to believe in fairies and to meet them,
yet deep down we fear this can never be.

This ache to delve into the world of fairies isn't new. People have been intrigued by fairies since the beginning of time. Even now in our high-tech world, a desire to discover more about fairies is there at the back of our overworked minds. We still tell fairy stories to fill quiet moments and calm tired children, to leave the stress and busyness of everyday life behind. Have you noticed that when we immerse ourselves in fairy tales, we feel a sudden deep longing to inhabit a more enchanted space? To live in a kingdom wiser and kinder than our own?

Many people yearn to connect with fairies, yet fear deep down this can never be. Talk of fairies doesn't quite seem to fit in with our 24/7 lifestyles, with a new world which only values what it can see and touch. Too often, this narrow view leaves us believing that any talk of fairies is childish, fanciful or out of reach.

Yet just a few decades ago, adults talked freely about fairies, of their own fairy encounters and of the importance of respecting the work fairies do. It's sad that those who still enjoy a relationship with fairies rarely speak about their remarkable experiences for fear of ridicule.

It's no coincidence that this disconnection with all things 'fairy' comes at a time when we are struggling to find meaningful ways to relate to each other and to nature. When we view fairy tales purely as make-believe, we let go of endless possibilities for enchantment, and condemn ourselves to lesser lives. I know this because I've experienced firsthand the deep sadness that comes when life closes in.

We carry in our cells the sweet memory of happier times,
when our ancestors and fairies were close,
and what was once can be so again.

Many of those who live close to the earth still have precious fairy stories in their keeping. Their tales are not born of wild imaginings, but come from direct contact with fairies. Those in touch with the earth know the fairy world is real, because they've been surprised and enchanted by fairy folk of all descriptions. That's why it's not difficult for those people to honour the work fairies do, and why in turn the fairies reward their loving attention by sharing some of their many secrets.

Fairies have existed alongside humankind since time began. Some say it was fairies who brought us the gift of fire, who showed us how to work with metal. That it was the fairy folk who first taught us the beauty of song and dance, music and poetry. That it was these enchanting beings who first revealed the healing power of plants and trees. I've no idea whether this is so, but I have no doubt fairies exist and that their task is to help life thrive in all its forms. Without their assistance, it would have been much harder for our ancestors to survive in deserts and mountain terrain, in the lands of ice and snow.

So where does this leave us? When we come adrift from nature and her fairy caretakers, we miss out on countless possibilities to taste life's many enchantments. Yet it needn't be this way. Each of us carries in our cells the sweet memory of happier times, when our ancestors and the fairies were close. Back then, we had a greater love of the earth and took better care of its many creatures. And what was once can be ours again.

SOME DAY YOU WILL BE OLD ENOUGH TO
START READING FAIRY TALES AGAIN.[1]

C S Lewis

Sensing Fairies

When I was little, it was easier to believe in fairies and the daily magic they wove. Just to think of fairies filled me with delight. But as I grew, my interest in fairies waned. So too did my sense of wonderment. Now it saddens me to think of all the years I ignored this deeper connection with nature. Looking back, I can see how much harder life was as a result. It's not so much that fairies were invisible to me, I'd simply lost my ability to sense them. On a deeper level, I'd come adrift from the fabric of life; while I was 'successful', I walked the world as a stranger.

Fairies reach out to you in the caress
of the wind on your cheek,
in the sudden biting cold of a winter's morning.

Later, when I began to seek fairies out, life started to soften and open up. I began to realise I wasn't alone. I saw how fairies reach out to us constantly, in all kinds of ways. In the plaintive cry of a bird. In an achingly lovely flower. In the caress of the wind on one's cheek. In the sudden biting cold of a winter's morning. In these and a thousand other ways fairies seek to inspire us, to help us give voice to something much deeper than we can access in everyday life. Fairies reach out to all that is soulful in us. They speak to us in beautiful moments and experiences, because beauty is a richer, more healing language than our own.

As I started to seek out fairies, to understand their world, I began by immersing myself in nature. The more time I spent there, the more it was where I wanted to be. I found myself aching to breathe in fresh air, to take a stroll in the park, to appreciate neighbourhood trees and gardens, to collect fallen twigs, feathers and leaves. As I did so, life began to shift for me in all kinds of unexpected ways. I felt more balanced. More peaceful too. I discovered that time in nature, even small snatches of time, had a profound effect on me. As I immersed myself in these small moments of beauty, my doubts and fears began to dissolve. I began to feel more optimistic. To see and appreciate how immensely lovely and sacred life is.

Yet as inspiring as these moments were, there was so much more I needed to understand. I began to realise that despite the many ways we continue to harm the earth, the fairies haven't given up on us. They still try to commune with us, as they have so much to share. But it's hard to get our attention, as so many of us are distracted most of the time. That's why fairies choose to appear one minute and vanish the next. It's their way of trying to wake us up, to help us feel fully alive. Sometimes the only way fairies can speak to us is in our dreams and daydreams, when we finally soften and relax. Fairies also love to draw close to us in the sweet drowsiness between waking and sleep. They love the luminous possibilities of these kinds of liminal space. Sometimes they make use of moments of extreme tiredness, when we're more open, less resistant.

Frequently, fleet-footed fairies come to us when we least expect them, surprising and delighting us, trying to help lift us out of our anxiety, our despair. While fairies don't wrestle with the many issues we humans do, they're very aware of how much our emotions weigh heavily on us. They draw close to uplift us. To offer us a little more of life's magic. To help heal those parts of us that are broken, so that together we can take better care of each other and this tiny jewel of a planet.

Sometimes the only way fairies can reach us is in our dreams and daydreams, when finally we soften and relax.

So where are fairies to be found? What do they look like? Many describe fairies as fireflies or tiny pinpricks of light. Some talk of their rapid movements being like a hummingbird's wings. Others experience fairies as sudden movements in their peripheral vision. There are no hard and fast rules about how fairies will appear, as they take on many forms. The important thing is to be open to the possibility of communing with them in some way.

When fairies do appear, you may think you're dreaming at first. I certainly did. My first experience of fairies as an adult was at a workshop that had nothing to do with fairies. The teacher had placed a small bunch of yellow roses on the table beside her. I don't know what drew my attention to them, but when I looked at the roses I saw a fairy smiling back at me from inside one of the roses. I was so astonished I'd no idea what to do. I simply stared back at this tiny being in disbelief. I even blinked a few times, but to my astonishment she was still there. It was a moment of pure happiness, of quiet bliss. Then my rational side kicked in.

I was convinced I was imagining the whole thing. Embarrassed, I looked away. Yet when I glanced back at the rose, this radiant little being was still there, smiling at me with such warmth and love. My fairy friend continued to smile at me from the centre of the rose for ten or more minutes. Then she vanished. I'm not sure why she made herself known to me, but whenever I think about her, I can still see her loving face and feel her sweet radiance.

One of the many gifts of fairy encounters is how the astonishing luminosity of a single fairy moment or experience remains with us, enabling us to draw on that loving energy and wisdom over time, even years later. All this and more is possible.

Reaching Out to Our Fairy Friends

So how can you see fairies? When and where are they most likely to appear? Wasn't this what our child self ached to know? And what many of us still do?

Before looking at powerful ways to reach out to the fairy kingdom, it's important to realise that you already have a connection to the world of the fairies. More than that, every inspired moment you've had in nature means you've already touched their breathtaking world. Think back to a beautiful sunset you've experienced, or that sudden glimpse of a snow-capped mountain or stretch of ocean. Do you remember how that single moment filled you with delight? Do you recall how your whole being expanded with joy? Do you remember how, for an instant, any heaviness you may have been experiencing vanished? How you felt there was nothing you could not do? That's because in one luminous moment, your soul connected with the healing power of the fairy kingdom.

It's astonishing to realise there's not a person on the planet who hasn't tasted the heady beauty of the fairy world. What's even more exciting is that many more luminous experiences await you. The more consciously you make these connections, the more you will benefit from the healing and wisdom they offer.

So how best to connect with our fairy friends? One of the most effective ways to create a meaningful relationship with fairies is to create your own special link to the fairy realm. You can do this by becoming more aware of your surroundings whenever you're in nature. Take in a specific tree. Examine its leaves and branches, the shape and texture of any flowers. And what of its surroundings? Perhaps there are feathers or pebbles or mud on the path ahead. Note the surrounding colours. The quality of light. The smell of the earth. Take in the playful breeze. The warmth of the sun on your face. The presence of birds and insects. As you absorb these nuances, you widen your perceptions and begin to awaken to the living world around you, to build your very own bridge to the world of fairies.

Previous generations had little difficulty seeing fairies, partly because life was simpler and slower back then. People had time to note hundreds of tiny details in the living world around them, creating a very intimate connection to this realm beyond our own. Most of us live in towns and cities now. We spend our lives in our homes, at work or at the shopping mall. When outside, we're distracted by traffic and all the busyness around us, so the gifts we were born with lie dormant within us. As a result, we become disconnected from the living world and from our own inmost selves. That's why fairies are largely invisible to us.

Yet in spite of all the distractions we face, there is no need to despair. We can still see fairies, we just need to work a little harder at doing so. The first step is to balance out the fast pace and distraction of city life with a little time in nature each day, each week. Just a few moments immersed in nature can work wonders over time.

> *The fairy world is much more refined*
> *and fluid than our own.*

Connecting with nature helps us build a bridge to the fairies, as nature is where fairy folk are often found. Later we'll learn of less likely places where fairies dwell, but beginning with nature is a good starting point. As you set off on this exquisite journey, take care not to burden yourself with unrealistic expectations. Simply spend time in nature, tasting and taking note of whatever you find there. It may feel a little strange at first. It certainly did for me. But looking back, I can see that was simply because this path was unfamiliar.

At one stage I found myself way out of my comfort zone, when studying healing flower essences. During our time together, the teacher encouraged us to pay more attention to nature and to our own intuition. As I've lived largely in cities, I felt a bit intimidated by her suggestion. I didn't see myself as an overly intuitive person, as I didn't see auras or dead people. Looking back, it's not surprising I felt a bit uncomfortable. At that time my life was crammed full of meetings and deadlines, and when I finally switched off I was exhausted. Yet I really wanted to learn about the essences, so I was motivated to give my intuition a go.

One of the first exercises the teacher gave was for each of us to go outside, choose a flower and draw it. I liked this idea, until she suggested we try to communicate with the flower. This seemed really way out to me at the time. My first impulse was to head for the hills. Yet I also knew I'd never be able to communicate with flowers unless I tried. Heading outside, I wandered around the garden in a daze. I was convinced the whole thing was a waste of time, until I came across a little white flower. I was immediately drawn to its beauty, its delicacy, its gentle energy. It seemed like the perfect flower to practise on. Settling down, I studied this tiny flower and began to draw it. As I started to relax, I was surprised to find myself enjoying the whole process, and was drawn deeper into the flower's loving energy.

As a tangible sense of love and appreciation began to flow between myself and the flower, I felt like I'd just made a wonderful new friend. I began to connect to the flower in ways I'd never experienced before. I was mesmerised by its stamens. By the way the flower's tiny petals came together. I couldn't believe how much fun I was having and found myself wanting to discover everything about the flower.

Try not to get caught up in your need
to have a fairy experience,
because no-one, not even fairies, likes needy.

By the time I tried to commune with the flower, it seemed the most natural thing ever. To my surprise, the flower answered instantly. Telepathically. As our 'conversation' got going, I was blown away by how much this flower knew about what was happening at the course and beyond it. We 'talked' about many things. As I was on a bit of a roll, I couldn't resist asking the flower for its take on my life. I was amazed at how accurately it described how overwhelmed I was. This was true—work was really challenging at the time, as our company was in the middle of a takeover. The insights this little flower shared were spot on. By the time the teacher called us back inside, I was sorry to leave my little flower behind. The flower essences course had many such moments, sensitising me to the living world on a whole new level.

In the weeks and months that followed, I began to see my surroundings very differently from the way my busy city self tended to look at things. When I was out in the fresh air, I found myself slowing down a little and softening my gaze. As I did so, I started to notice how a certain tree swayed in the wind; the colour of its leaves after rain. I delighted in the slow progress a snail made across my path; in an unexpected patch of daffodils in a nearby miniature garden. With these tiny discoveries came a real sense of the wonder of nature in all her hues. It left me less stressed and more blessed. At the time, I'd no idea these tiny steps would help me connect to fairies.

It was later that I came to see how nature provides us with dozens of stepping stones to the fairy realms. I discovered that 'lightness of being' is also essential, if we want to develop a relationship with fairies. Light is another essential ingredient, as fairies live in a world that is lighter, more refined and more fluid than our own. So whenever you're able to 'lighten up' a little, you naturally draw closer to the light-filled world of fairies, which in turn makes it easier for you to experience them.

Following these steps doesn't mean you'll automatically see fairies. Not everyone does. But you will be able to sense them. If you're serious about wanting to experience fairies, it also helps to believe in them. Fairies don't have time to waste on those whose eyes and hearts are shut. So allow for the possibility that fairies may just be real. Welcome them into your world.

Love is another essential ingredient to seeing fairies,
because love helps dissolve the barriers
between us, and opens the door to a world of
unparalleled beauty and wonderment.

Spending time in nature will also help you to lighten up. So whenever you are in nature, it's important to try to leave your worries behind. As you relax, you're more able to immerse yourself in your surroundings. Try not to get caught up in your need to have a fairy experience, because no-one—not even fairies—likes needy. Simply delight in all the nuances around you. A small stone or feather. A towering tree.

When you take this approach you begin to love what you're seeing and experiencing. This is perfect, as love is another essential ingredient to seeing fairies. Love helps dissolve the barriers between humans and fairies, opening the door to a world of unparalleled beauty and wonderment.

As I began to immerse myself in nature, to notice the way the sun lingered on the horizon or how the sky looked before a winter storm, I forgot about my need to see fairies. In its place came an openness to simply discover what my time in nature might bring. And as we'll see, I experienced far more than I could have hoped for.

So when next there's a sudden stray wind around you when everything else is still, or you catch an unexpected hint of a flower's perfume, these and a thousand other details are telling you that the fairies are less than a heartbeat away.

Inside the Fairy Realm

As so few people talk about fairies these days, it's easy to assume
no-one sees them. But that's not so. I've been amazed at the
number of people who have seen fairies and continue to do so.
What is fascinating about their accounts is how much they reveal
about fairies. 'My fairies did not have bodies,' recalls Celia, now
in her nineties. 'They were just there as beings, life-energy beings
seen inwardly as light, but not to be compared to the dull light
that comes from light bulbs.'

Writer and seer, Rosemary Guiley, often saw fairies around
her as sparkling balls of light. When she lived in Connecticut,
Rosemary liked to gaze out at the trees at dusk. 'During these
reveries, I became aware of silvery-white lights that either floated
or shot quickly around,' she tells. 'I noticed the lights especially at
times when I was in a peaceful mood, not thinking of anything in
particular, but simply drinking in the beauty, scents and sounds

of the environment around me. On moonlit nights, the woods were magical with lights. I also noticed the lights at dawn.'[2]

The fairy realms are brimful with enchantment.

Many speak of the radiance of fairies. As we're so used to the everyday world around us, it's hard to imagine just how dazzling is the space occupied by fairies. When we do compare their light-filled realm with our world of bricks and mortar, our immediate environment seems heavy and constricted by comparison. Far too many of us have become so used to the endless round of working, shopping and commuting that it's hard to imagine what may lie beyond this. That's why we seek comfort from the things we can see and touch, or rely on material possessions to help us feel safe or even powerful. Yet as reassuring as everyday things may appear, one of the messages fairies have is for us to take care, lest the material world and its many comforts end up imprisoning us.

Fairies are at pains to remind us that our world, which seems so solid and secure, is in fact an exquisite dance of tiny particles. And that here in this ocean of particles, life is pure radiance, pure light. Like the fairies, you and I can access this radiance if we so choose. One of the best ways to experience the radiance is to raise our life energy to match the refined energy of the fairy realms. You can do this by cultivating a lightness of being. Nature also helps us to lighten up. So step outside and breathe in the fresh air, walk in the park, the mountains or the woods, until you feel yourself coming alive again.

*Making this transition from our everyday
world to the fairy realms
is about seeing the world as sacred, and appreciating the
daily miracles, large and small, that come our way.*

Many of us spend our lives sitting still or scarcely moving. It's become a way of life. It wasn't until I began to spend time out in nature that things changed for me. My exhaustion and cynicism lifted. My life energy soared. Then, as my everyday worries and responsibilities dissolved, I began to soften and heal. As a lighter, more radiant me emerged, life began to sparkle again.

I started to appreciate the world as the miracle it is. To see that rocks and pebbles, grains of sand and the waves in the ocean are every bit as alive as you or I. When you experience this level of aliveness, you step into the enchanted slipstream of life. Once there, you're able to access whole new levels of beauty, insight and inspiration in a small bird or wayside flower, in the soft whisper of a breeze. So why not make time to visit the places in nature you love? Allow them to energise you, to lift your spirits and feed your soul.

When you step out of your routine, you begin to experience the beauty within and beyond our everyday world. To see just how sacred life is. You touch the essence of life, a place that is exquisitely lovely with limitless wisdom, which connects you with all that is truly divine. It is here in the midst of this loveliness that fairies reside. Once you establish a heightened connection with nature, nothing seems ordinary anymore. Your heart rejoices to see a shimmering red sun dissolve into the sea, to hear the dry rustle of leaves on a chill breeze, or to discern the whisper of a mighty ocean in a tiny shell.

As you drink in this beauty and allow it to inspire you, you'll see life for the miracle it is. And touched by this sense of wonder, you'll draw closer to the fairies, as they inhabit a world of miracles. One of the secrets to making this transition is to let go of your desire to see fairies. Simply gaze deep into a flower or watch the sunlight catch a single dewdrop. Allow these and other sights and sounds bring you alive again and lead you to places you never thought possible.

Less Than a Heartbeat Away

You can always tell when fairies are close by. Suddenly everything comes into sharp focus. The air shimmers. The colours are more intense. The rocks, plants and trees seem more real, more distinct. You feel as if you're seeing the world for the very first time. It's as if you have lived your whole life in black and white, and suddenly everything is blazing with colour.

This heightening of the senses is hard to explain, because we don't have the words for it, but you'll know it when it happens. The moment may be quite subtle for you, but dramatic too, because you're moving way beyond your everyday experiences. This is where it starts to get really exciting!

Fairies speak to us in beautiful moments and experiences, because beauty is a richer, more healing language than our own.

When there's a sudden intensity in what you're seeing and feeling in your surroundings, when your senses are heightened to levels never experienced before, you'll know you're onto something. You can't mistake this feeling, because you feel so alive. This intensity, this aliveness, indicates that for a fleeting moment you are seeing or experiencing your immediate surroundings to a level never previously achieved. This shimering space is bursting with potential. This is the space where the fairies live and work. A place that is many more times healing and inspiring than our own.

So what does this heightening of the senses feel like? The first time this happened to me was a sunny afternoon several years ago. I was having lunch in a local park. As I settled down on the grass, the atmosphere became suddenly electric. In an instant, I was filled with a massive sense of anticipation, the way I'd felt on Christmas Eve when I was little. I just knew something out of the ordinary was about to happen. No sooner had I noticed this change in atmosphere, when I found myself staring down at the grass in disbelief. I'd never seen grass so green! Its colour and vibrancy literally took my breath away.

As I gazed around in wonderment, I realised it wasn't just the colour of the grass that was so amazing. I was also experiencing the life force of the hundreds of thousands of blades of grass. Their life force pulsed through me like an electric current. It felt exhilarating and peaceful at the same time. In that instant I felt part of every single blade of grass, and of the whole living world. Alive doesn't even get close to the entirety of the feeling I had. It was like sticking my fingers into a cosmic light socket. It was one of the most exquisite moments of my life.

I've no idea how long this incident lasted, but I'll never forget the astonishing sense of belonging and beauty that enfolded me. Here I was taking a few moments out from a busy day in the office in a city of millions to have my lunch. Yet at the same time I was somewhere else altogether. It was as if I'd stepped into another world. One that was more lovely, more complete than our own. The remarkable thing was that I was still aware of the everyday world, except it was nowhere near as vivid. It had faded to the point of not seeming quite real.

You can always tell when fairies are close by,
because everything comes into sharp focus.

Looking back, I realise I'd glimpsed our world the way fairies see it. At its shimmering essence. It was another space altogether. One that was far more vibrant, more lovely than anything we experience in everyday life. I now know that this is the space fairies occupy all the time.

This incident was life-changing. Years later, it's impossible to forget how exquisite and uncomplicated life felt in those few brief moments. Every time I think of that incident, I can still recapture a little of its magic. In that momentary flash, I got a taste of how life can be. Not just for me, but for all of us. That little miracle will never be forgotten. It helps warm up those moments when I feel tired or down. It also stretched my sense of what's possible.

This, I've discovered, is what the fairy realms do. They help connect us more profoundly to ourselves and to the whole of life. They help put us in the frame of mind and frequency to attract miracles, large and small.

In many ways, what happened to me in the park isn't anything out of the ordinary. These 'quickening' moments in nature happen all the time. It's just that most of us spend little time in nature, so the opportunity to experience such lovely possibilites are few and far between. Yet in spite of our stress and busyness, the opportunities to glimpse living nature and her fairy caretakers is still there for us, if we make an effort to get outside. My lunch-time experience made me realise just how crucial time in nature is. Being out in the fresh air in a park, in the woods, or walking by the ocean allows the fog of everyday life to lift. Then as we shed our concerns, another part of us emerges that is wiser, more perceptive, more open, and more likely to let the fairy world in.

You don't have to be in a remote place to cross between worlds. You can do this wherever there's a tiny patch of nature in your town or city. All you need do is take time out to visit your neigh-bourhood park or beach. Make the effort to venture a little further afield. To stroll through a forest, by a lake or wherever in nature you're inspired to be. It's important you get to know and love the places you visit and that while you're there, you give them your full attention, just as you would for someone you care about. Your love and attention are essential, as they help build a bridge between our everyday world and the world of the fairies. Then 'heightened' moments like the one I've just described may well follow.

The secret is not to get caught up in your need to see fairies.

It's interesting to listen to other people's experiences of their special crossover moments, as it helps us know what to look for. Joy told of the same intensifying of her senses when she was out enjoying a carefree stroll. 'It was a bright sunny, calm after-noon. I'd been walking for about fifteen minutes when I became aware that the wind had picked up a little,' she recalls. 'I actually heard the wind first and, for whatever reason, I looked up and noticed that the trees along my route were very animated. They were swaying back and forth, and I noticed all their features, the leaves, trunk etc, were almost magnified. It was like they wanted me to notice the detail. Everything else, from sky to streetscape, seemed to fade into the background. I saw the trees in a completely different way to how I would normally look at a tree. I was mesmerised for about ten seconds, then I looked back to the path to check where I was walking. When I looked back up, you might say everything was back to normal. The wind had gone. The trees were no longer swaying. They were back to how they always look—not three dimensional and in-your-face, as they had been.'

When these crossover incidents occur, you never forget them. They're so astonishingly vibrant it feels like you've just witnessed the first day of creation, a world that's hugely more colourful, more comforting than our own. Having experienced this other world, you ache for further uplifting experiences. Suddenly you find yourself savouring the sweet dampness of the earth, reaching out and touching wayside plants or trees, breathing the scent of a flower deep into your being, running your fingers reverentially over a leaf, or picking up a stone or stray feather that demands your attention. Be assured that whenever you respond lovingly to nature, you naturally draw additional exquisite moments your way, which may just include a fairy or two.

Robert Ogilvie Crombie, who was very close to the Findhorn community in Scotland in its fledgling years, was no stranger to moments of heightened awareness when out in nature. He also believed that this change in atmosphere was one of the many signs that fairies were close by. 'I felt a great build-up of power and a vast increase in awareness,' he explains. 'Colours and forms became more significant. I was aware of every single leaf on the bushes and trees; every blade of grass on the path was standing out with startling clarity. It was as if physical reality had become much more real than it normally is, and the three-dimensional effect we are used to had become even more solid.'[3] Robert Ogilvie Crombie, or Roc as he was known, had a scientific background and liked to check things out, which meant he was able to capture his fairy experiences in wonderful detail. One of his great legacies is the many detailed descriptions he left of his time with the fairies. 'There was an acute feeling of being one with nature in a complete way, as well as being one with the divine, which produced great exultation, and a deep sense of wonder and awe,'[4] he reflects.

The next time you feel sad, confused or lonely,
go for a walk in the woods, beside a lake,
or along a beach, knowing the fairies are also there.

When you have such exquisite moments, suddenly your everyday ups and downs don't seem as important. These extraordinary incidents help you experience what it's like to be whole. You get to see yourself as you really are, a beautiful valued part of creation. Then, as you come back into balance, some wounded part of you is healed.

So next time you feel sad, lonely or confused, go for a walk in the woods, beside a lake or along a beach, knowing the fairies are there with you. When you reach the woods or meadows, or wherever in living nature you choose to be, don't get caught up in expectations of what might happen. Simply relax. Let go of everything that's worrying you or taking up your time. Just let it dissolve until you feel as light and delicate as mist. Then as the everyday world fades, it's the perfect time to reach out to the living world that enfolds you.

When you can move beyond your need to see fairies, you're more open to any or all of the remarkable things that might happen. How, you ask, can you help this process along? The secret is to start to gaze about you with a gentle, loving eye. Begin to take note of your immediate surroundings—of anything and everything that catches your eye without judgement. Stay relaxed. Gently remind yourself that you are a part of nature. Pay attention to the tiniest details, from the brightly coloured stamens at the heart of a flower, to the joyous dips and swirls of a swallow as it catches the breeze.

These details are precious, because they feed and enlighten the soul. Because it's in these silken moments you help draw the fairies to you. Fairies use nature's beauty to help capture your attention. It is they who invite you to breathe in the deep green of plants and leaves, to lose yourself in the brilliant blue of the sky. So drink in all the loveliness you can. And know that every little nuance will help you see and experience more of this enchanted world, which exists alongside our own. Don't force or hurry this process. Just savour everything in nature you're naturally drawn to, large and small.

Through nature's beauty, the fairies invite
you to embrace life in its fullness,
to breathe in the deep green of the plants and leaves,
to lose yourself in the brilliant blue of the sky

These simple steps may seem hardly worth the effort, but they are truly magical. If you want to make this transition from our everyday world to the light-filled realms of the fairies, you need to develop a heightened awareness of life, to experience the subtleties of nature. Then, as you allow your senses to lead you wherever in nature your spirit needs to go, you will start to build a bridge to the luminous world of fairies, which is subtle and delicate beyond imagining.

So when next you are out in nature, let go of your everyday concerns and relax. Allow your heart to fill with love, to be in the moment. Don't hesitate to run your hands over the smooth roundness of a rock. To bathe your face in dewdrops. To kick off your shoes and dance on bare earth. To let the sun-scorched sand slip through your fingers. Do whatever inspires, so that your soul can begin to sing again.

SOME SAY THAT WHEN A PERSON DOESN'T
BELIEVE IN FAIRIES, A FAIRY DIES.
THIS ISN'T SO. WHEN YOU SAY SUCH THINGS,
SOMETHING INSIDE YOU DIES.
IT BECOMES MUCH HARDER TO
EXPERIENCE LIFE'S DEEP MAGIC.

When Children See Fairies

When I was little, seeing fairies was a perfectly normal part of childhood. No doubt it helped that children spent hours alone in nature, climbing trees, exploring woods and seashores, gathering up any little treasures they came across. Back then, there was more time to dig in the earth and play in the sand, to gaze up at clouds, to develop a lasting connection with the living world and its fairy caretakers. Nowadays, our children spend little time outside, so these priceless opportunities to connect with fairies are fast disappearing. I cannot help think we are poorer for it.

I first saw fairies when I was in my special tree.
They were very little glittering figures,
just like the drawings you see.

LUCILLE

This doesn't mean that children no longer see fairies, just that it's just harder for many to do so. In talking with those who saw fairies as children, I began to appreciate how much of an affinity fairies have for the young. It doesn't matter whether it's tiny seedlings, little creatures or small children, fairies seem to delight in the promise of new life. They also love the innocence of childhood, and the freedom it offers for little ones to explore the world around them. I also suspect fairies have less difficulty in relating to young children, because children are more open and less distracted.

One of the most moving discoveries I made, when talking to people about their childhood experiences, was the very real difference the presence of fairies made to a child's life. I was astonished to learn about the level of joy and soul nourishment children received from fairies.

Lucille, a busy grandmother who sees fairies, grew up in the country, where she spent a lot of time alone in nature. She has no doubt that all that time in nature helped her see these luminous beings. 'I would spend a lot of time wandering around the family farm on my own,' she tells. 'We had no TV or anything else, so we just wandered around outside. I first saw fairies when I was in my special tree. They were very little glittering figures, just like in the drawings you see. Their wings were fluttering so fast they were like a bee's wings. I didn't have any communication with them when I was little. They just flew around.'

Hearing of Lucille's early years, you could be forgiven for assuming hers was an idyllic childhood, but this wasn't so. Lucille witnessed a neighbour's murder when she was small. Yet as traumatic as this was, Lucille's abiding memory of her early years is of the delight and reassurance that her fairy encounters brought her.

When Lucille was ten she was given *Peg's Fairy Book*, which was full of wonderful fairy drawings. Lucille was thrilled to see that these fairies were just like the fairies she saw around flowers. 'The pictures were like sitting in fairyland, which was exactly how I saw things,' she recalls.

Lucille has continued to see fairies over the years, as have some of the children who wander past her home. 'Ten to fifteen years ago, I used to see fairies in my garden, but I don't see them so much now,' Lucille admits. 'They were just flitting around the flowers and the bushes. The kids who went past my place used to say I had fairies in my garden as well. And the parents used to tell me what their children had said, so I used to invite their children into the garden.'

There are numerous ways fairies appear to children. Each encounter leaves its mark, reminding children of life's magic. 'My first fairy sighting was at ten,' explains Linda, who now works in a busy literary agency. 'My stepfather had designed and built a beautiful three-tiered pond in the backyard of our new house. The water would trickle down the levels into the fish pond, and I decorated the rock surroundings with small statues of pixies and seashells. I would sit in the backyard, staring at this magical place. It was so beautiful. So many summer days were spent fixated on the pond, while I watched the sprinklers send a spray of mist over it all. The sun would shine through the mist, creating a rainbow of light. How could anyone tire of that?

'I'd been playing in our backyard pool and the sprinklers had just been turned on, when I saw her. A shimmer of light in the form of a small female darted through the gaps of water. Skipping in between the small plants, she disappeared near the pond— my pond. My first reaction was to freeze, my mouth open. It was as though my feet were stuck to the grass. Then I was off. I ran back into the house so quickly, screaming at the top of my voice that I'd just seen a fairy in the garden!

'My mother's response was something like, "Really? You're a lucky girl." Of course, that didn't reduce my excitement. I went on and on about what I had seen. I remember a gold blur of light. It seemed to jump a short distance before stopping and becoming the shape of a tiny female. Her form was slight and her hair long. This being was lit up in silver, gold and small fragments of colour. There was a fine light beam, creating what appeared to be wings behind her arms. She looked behind her and, as quickly as she had appeared she was gone, disappearing almost instantly as she leapt toward the rocks.'

It seems that fairies take great delight in surprising and enchanting children, and lifting them up when they feel down. After falling sick with a bad case of the mumps, Kim was stuck inside. Things weren't looking great, as the family vacation was fast approaching. Everyone was staying out of poor Kim's way. Then one day, as she was staring across the room at the stained-glass windows above the family piano, Kim caught sight of two small pale yellow-green figures, less than a foot tall. They were bent over laughing and pointing at her. She remembers their long limbs, pointy fingers and big almond-shaped eyes. These two fairies wore soft pointy hats and shoes.

Looking at these fairies closely, Kim couldn't help but notice how different their energy was compared to humans. This observation is something many people who encounter fairies comment on. 'Everything about them was subtle, no sharply-defined edges or colours,' she recalls. 'They looked exactly the same.' Kim ended up staring at these two little figures for a long time, then remembers falling asleep. 'It was one of those moments you never forget,' she relates.[5]

Fairies have a great affinity for the young.
Whether it's tiny seedlings, little creatures or small children,
fairies delight in the promise of new life.

One of the reasons why childhood is so magical is that children believe in the possibility of magic and that dreams can come true. And if they're lucky, fairies can help make this happen, as Niomi discovered when she was five. After losing her first tooth, Niomi's dad read her a story about tooth fairies and a child who'd been taken to fairyland in a blanket. Hearing this enchanting tale, little Niomi really wished the same thing would happen to her. Then curiously, when she fell asleep that night, she remembers being lifted up in a blanket. She recalls a 'floating feeling', as well as the 'rippling of the blanket' and the 'wind rushing' over her face. At one point Niomi tried to open her eyes, but was unable to do so. Then she experienced a sudden thump, as if she'd been dropped, and woke up to find herself back in bed. Again, this lovely incident lingers in Niomi's memory.[6]

Dreams are the perfect way for fairies to make contact, because it's much easier to get our attention when we're asleep. Fairies can comfort us here too, as little Dior discovered after breaking her beautiful Christmas snow dome. Dior was devastated at the time, but then some fairies came to her rescue in a reassuring dream. 'I broke something really precious,' Dior explains. 'When I went to sleep in the middle of the night they came to visit me in my bedroom. The fairies made a fairy ring for me, because I was very upset about my snow dome. In the middle of the fairy ring was a brand new snow dome, almost exactly the same as the Santa one I had broken.' Seeing the new snow dome in her dream helped Dior deal with her upset and disappointment.

Some fairies can be extremely mischievous, as Celia discovered when a group of 'prickly, woolly little gnomes' appeared amid several thorny gooseberry bushes in her childhood garden. They struck up a friendship with her. 'They encouraged me and my friends to eat too many gooseberries, especially unripe ones,' she recalls with a wry smile. 'How they would giggle in their cheeky ways when they saw the effect that unripe berries had on our tummies!'

Dreams are the perfect way for fairies to make contact.

Sometimes fairy encounters are more than a little mystifying, and can never be fully explained. In what she describes as 'the very strangest day in my life', Carissa was surprised to find a fairy with a purple dress following her to school. She was even more shocked to discover this fairy in her bedroom when she got home. The fairy seemed to be talking to Carissa, but she couldn't understand what the fairy was saying. Carissa was concerned that perhaps the fairy's wings were broken. She rang her mother who didn't believe her, so Carissa had sort things out for herself. Returning to her room she was relieved to see the fairy's wings were fine. The fairy smiled at Carissa and gave her a small bag of what looked like sand, then flew off. Carissa had no idea what it all meant, but it's an incident she'll never forget.[7]

Sarah was also extremely surprised to see a fairy one night when no-one else was around. Glancing up at her bookcase, she was 'pretty shocked' to see a fairy with medium blonde hair staring back at her. This fairy was floating in midair with one hand on Sarah's bookcase, wearing a green dress with red and white striped stockings. Her wings were moving very slowly, and low enough for Sarah to see her Orlando Bloom poster through the fairy's wings. Thinking she was hallucinating, Sarah kept on blinking, expecting the fairy to disappear, but it stayed with her until she went to bed.

Sometimes fairies want to be noticed and sometimes they don't. It had been raining a lot when Jordan saw a sudden splash in the school pond. When he took a closer look, he was surprised to see a tiny figure with 'webbed wings' there. Another time he was walking across the road to a nearby creek when he passed a plant with a striking dark purple flower. Intrigued, Jordan looked more closely at the flower and was surprised to see a fairy face staring back at him. Once the fairy realised it had been seen, it 'vanished into thin air' along with the plant.

All of these stories are intriguing. It's tempting to dismiss these incidents as cute stories with little relevance to our fast-paced lives. But as we'll see, fairy encounters can have a profound impact on children. Fairies do help some children cope with their everyday worries or a deep sadness, or in some cases with abuse.

Fairy Nurture

Until people began relating their childhood experiences of fairies to me, I'd never appreciated how much fairies help some children settle into life here on earth. I was deeply moved by some of the tales people told of fairies saving the day for them in otherwise difficult childhoods.

Douglas, a retired customs officer in his late eighties, will never forget how much fairies brought to his early years. Growing up in Scotland in the shadow of the Great Depression, he had a challenging time as a boy. Jobs and food were scarce, and his family struggled to survive. One of Douglas' great comforts as a small boy was his time spent with the fairies at the bottom of his grandmother's garden. It was here Douglas would retreat when life was tough, spending many happy hours with his fairy friends. The fairies would laugh and play with Douglas, until he no longer felt frightened or sad. There's no doubt in Douglas' mind that the fairies warmed his tough early years, and helped instil in him a lifelong love of nature.

From the beginning of time, fairies have helped children settle into earthly life.

Half a world away, Sharon grew up in a privileged Jewish home where, in spite of material comforts, she frequently experienced physical abuse. 'By the time I was four I was fairly outspoken and argumentative, which shook my mother,' Sharon explains. 'She would often lash out and hit me across the head. I'd frequently have ringing in my ears. I never ran away, but when it was over I'd go into the garden where there were some little steps with a tree overhanging them. I'd sit on the steps under the hibiscus tree, watching the ants. It was like a little cave, because the branches were right over the steps.

'I don't know exactly when, but a being appeared to me—a golden woman, who became my secret. She'd talk to me for hours, and would give me a sense that I was a lovely person, and that everything would turn out well. She stayed with me until my grandmother died, when I was eleven. She had long golden curls and a long golden dress, and she shimmered. Just before she disappeared for the last time, she told me to always look to the stars. So when my grandmother died some time later, I looked up and chose a star for her. I would often look up at that star. It helped me feel close to my grandmother.'

Looking back, Sharon can't imagine what childhood would have been like without the comfort of her fairy friend.

Some fairies appeared very small and others,
such as the tree fairies, looked huge to me.
The fairies who were connected with the
roses and flowers felt closer to my size.

CELIA

Swiss-born Celia, now in her nineties, also had a difficult start. She lost her mother before her first birthday. The fairies proved a great comfort to Celia. 'Our house and garden was on the outskirts of Zurich,' she explains. 'We moved there when I was four. The garden had a wide open lawn with an old apple tree, two blue spruce trees, three tall white birch trees and many flowerbeds. It was there I encountered the fairies. Each was unique. Some fairies appeared very small and others, such as the tree fairies, looked huge to me—even higher than the blue spruces or the tall white birches. I did not just accept their presence without question, but indeed felt a great love for their unique personalities and characteristics. The fairies who were connected with the roses and flowers felt closer to my size. It was these fairies and the ones living under the trees and bushes I mostly played with. We played cheerful children's games together and I never felt lonely.

'The fairies and I made up many games together, mostly spontaneous games. Sometimes we would act out stories, where I provided the stage props in my mind and the fairies happily joined in, bringing my ideas to life. They laughed at having to "buy tickets" for the performances of plays I'd made up from my picture books of fairy tales by Grimm and Andersen. The most active play was with the many fairies who lived under the spruce trees. At one stage, I created a large imaginary swimming pool. They amused themselves by diving deep into the water and splashing about happily, then flying high up in the air.

'Seeing the fairies dancing around the trees and shrubs, and floating in and out of the branches of trees high in the air, was always just sheer delight. I certainly felt part of the merriment, of their beauty and elegance of movement. I often joined in their rhythmical, tuneful dances. Even as a small child I had a passion for dancing, and often took the opportunity of my family's absence from the house at night to dance by myself to the music from gramophone records or to my own songs.

'It was more exciting though to dance with the fairies, because they encouraged and inspired me with their joyousness. There was always happiness and laughter in our play. We enjoyed each other's presence. I felt part of them, of their very essence, and they were part of me. I felt exhilarated by this uplifting oneness with the fairies, and through them with all nature. This unifying experience gave me an inner unshakable conviction of the inter-connectedness and interdependence of all beings, of life itself.'

Celia's recollections of her joyful play with the fairies brings so many lovely details to life. She even has clear memories of the music the fairies made. 'I realise that (whenever the fairies were around) there was always some kind of music in the air; graceful charming tunes they were, light and pleasant, in accord-ance with our games,' she recalls. 'I took these delightful sounds for granted. Whether they were heard out loud or in my mind, or both, I am not sure. Music was just a constant presence when I was with the fairies.'

I felt exhilarated by this uplifting oneness with the fairies, and through them with all nature.

CELIA

This lighthearted, imaginative world of spontaneous play that Celia shared with the fairies is a million miles away from the stressed-out world we're all too familiar with. It's interesting to see the immediate change in atmosphere Celia sensed when adults were around. 'The moment a grown-up entered the garden, or even just looked down from the balcony, the fairies disappeared in a split second,' Celia recalls, then goes on to explain why. 'Grown-ups felt too heavy and blind for the fairies. Adults often asked me what I was doing, just standing there spellbound.' Like so many children, Celia tried to share her experiences with the adults in her life only to be disappointed. 'The idea of fairies was immediately dismissed as fancy and childish behaviour, so I never mentioned my invisible playmates again.'

These wonderful experiences remind us of what's possible when our children get the chance to connect with fairies. But what happens, I wonder, to the many children who no longer have ready access to nature? What fun and nurture are they missing out on? I guess some parents may worry that a preoccupation with fairies could make their children too dreamy and unable to make their way in the world, but this wasn't what I saw in the people I spoke with.

Douglas survived the challenges of World War II, then took his young family to live on the other side of the world in New Zealand. Celia is now a grandmother and one of the wisest, most grounded women I know. Sharon is a noted Gestalt psychotherapist with her own practice, who teaches around the globe. What the fairies did for Douglas, Celia and Sharon was to open their hearts and minds to a world of wider possibilities. The fairies enabled them to move beyond their immediate hurts and worries, to taste life's wisdom and beauty.

As we start to see how hard nature and her fairy caretakers work to comfort our children and uplift their fledgling spirits, why would we not want to encourage this process? Why not walk with our little ones in the woods and play in the meadows? Why not encourage them to stare up at the clouds, moon and stars? Why not teach them the gifts of the seasons, so their time here (and ours) may be enriched?

IF YOU WANT THEM (CHILDREN) TO BE MORE
INTELLIGENT, READ THEM MORE FAIRY TALES.[8]

Albert Einstein

Time in Nature Matters

Not everyone sees fairies when they are children. However, many adults I meet who see fairies did spend a lot of time in nature during their childhood years. They've no doubt that spending time in nature helped connect them to the fairy realms. When I think back to my early years spent in nature, I start to appreciate how much it fed my body and soul. How it helped dissolve moments of sadness and kept my imagination alive. I now see that being immersed in beauty opened me up to the enchanted pathways of the fairies.

Fairies help inspire children to explore rock pools,
to gaze up at the near round moon,
to dance barefoot on the dew-drenched earth.

Fairies nourish our children in all kinds of ways. It's fairies who help interest children in stray feathers and unusual stones, in beautifully patterned shells and leaves. It is they who inspire children to explore rock pools, to dance in puddles and gaze up at the near round moon. Fairies encourage these and a thousand other connections with the living world, to help children feel more at home here, to feel more complete. For children lucky enough to have these experiences, a ready access to nature can make a real difference to their adult lives.

'As a child, I was really blessed to be out a lot in the woods where I saw lots of nymphs and things,' explains Sue, a young teacher and artist who spent her early years in Yugoslavia. 'I just loved being outside. I'd go out to the trees and the woods a lot. As we were in the mountains, there were creeks everywhere and hardly any neighbours. I lived this way for five years. I had a beautiful life. Coming to the other side of the world was a big shock. All the lovely woods were gone. Looking back, I feel really blessed that I had nature.' Sue treasures her early years, and can see how they created an ongoing love of nature in her, and helped connect her with fairies as an adult. Sue's access to nature and her fairy caretakers continues to inspire her in the good times, and help her cope with life's more difficult moments.

Children who spend time in nature gain so much there. They get used to their own company, to silence and space between their thoughts. These experiences are a wonderful counterbalance to the full-on lives they may well lead as adults. Children brought up in this way are less likely to be bored with life. They're not afraid to have time on their own. And of course, fairy encounters are more likely in their future lives as well.

During Roshilla's time in nature as a child in Fiji, she first began to experience fairies. These enchanted moments still remain with her in her busy city life. 'As I was growing up, I felt there were a lot of beings around protecting me. This was good, as the environment I grew up in wasn't exactly safe,' this artist explains. 'I was very different to the other kids. Being in nature brought me a sense of wonderment. I could escape from all the harsh realities around me, and be where I felt safe. There was no pressure. I could just lose myself in that environment. It was the best thing, as I was very lonely growing up. It meant I could escape to somewhere where no-one would judge me. It was comforting to be outdoors. I found it very peaceful being in nature. I loved playing with the earth or running in the rice paddies. Just touching things in nature made me feel alive. I still have a sense of that magic as an adult,' she adds. 'It's very special, everyone should have that kind of access to nature in childhood.'

Mama, who has a German background, fondly recalls her early years immersed in the natural world, which led to some extraordinary experiences with fairies as an adult. 'Since I was a child, I have been enchanted with the natural world, feeling more at home in the woods and fields than any other place,' Mama reflects. 'I used to talk to the trees and flowers in the forest, and always felt some sort of presence when playing alone among the oaks, pines and wildflowers of my home.'

The same was true for Sarah, a young executive who grew up on a big country property in New Zealand. She can't imagine what her demanding city life would be like had she not spent her childhood in nature. 'I did a lot of things on my own,' she reflects. 'I'd go down to the stream to play, get lost in the tall grass, and play in the neighbour's haystacks. I was always alone in nature. It gave me a connection with the earth, with the soul of things.' Sarah regularly falls back on these early experiences, when city life and work pressures get too much. She believes these enchanting childhood years also paved the way for her fairy encounters as an adult. 'I feel quite sad for children who don't have this, because it connected me to myself,' she adds.

I was always alone in nature. It gave me a connection with the earth, with the soul of things.

SARAH

Now well into her eighties, Marian's contact with nature as a child came through time spent in a special garden. 'After all these years, I still dream about that garden,' she tells. 'It belonged to my mother's sister, who lived in a huge house with several bedrooms and a real garden. The place was magical. Children were allowed to play in the garden while the grown-ups drank tea and talked. It was a wonderful place. Full of mysterious flutterings and the many sounds of nature. Even then, I believed in the little people and almost saw them. I'd sense when they were close. There'd be a quick movement out of the corner of my eye, but I never turned quickly enough to catch a proper glimpse of them.

'At the bottom of the garden there was an apple tree. The apples were striped red and pale cream. They had the most delicious smell and taste. There were flowers and shrubs all around the lawn, and the lawn was dotted with daisies, which we were allowed to pick to make daisy chains. We enjoyed placing them on our heads and around our necks. It always seemed like summer when I was there. My lasting memory of the garden is of indescribable peace and warmth, and the perfume of different flowers. I've not seen the place in years, except when I go to sleep. Then the garden comes back to me, bringing me a deep sense of peace and happiness, and the recollection of those magical days with the little people.'

Walk with your children in the woods. Play in the meadows.
Lie on the ground and stare up at the clouds.
Take time to marvel at the moon and stars.

In these and other fairy experiences, children get their first taste of the enchantments of life. Not all children will see fairies during their childhood years, but by immersing themselves in nature they're building a connection with fairies regardless. 'I wasn't a fairy kid,' says Renee, a young graphic designer. 'We were tomboys, always outside. My parents lived on the river, so we'd fish, play in the mud and go camping.' Renee has no doubt that this time in nature helped pave the way for her experiences with the fairies later on. Though she didn't think much about fairies as a girl, they're now very much part of her life. 'I didn't see the fairy lights around people until the last few years,' she admits. 'But I now see them around people all the time.'

We should be grateful that the fairies try to immerse our little ones in a world of beauty, joy and nurture, before they have to deal with the more challenging aspects of life. It's heartening to see how much small children get out of their fairy encounters. 'Fairies like to collect nectar,' explains six-year-old Dior. 'They are very shy. They like playing hide-and-seek, because they are very good hiders. There are many different types of fairies. All the fairies I know are tree fairies, flower fairies, nature fairies, home fairies, sky fairies, ground fairies and river fairies. I know there are more, but I don't know all of them.' Dior describes the fairies she sees as 'very delicate and see-through, magical and able to fly. They're like bees, because they have stripes on them and they buzz,' she explains, adding, 'fairies also like honey, 'cos they like sweet things.'

Reflecting on these experiences, I cannot help but think a childhood spent in nature is a far more positive and stimulating world for our children than spending their early years in rooms full of toys and branded junk. Children need silence and space to get to know themselves and their world. To gain a true sense of belonging, they need to feel the ground beneath their feet and the wind in their hair.

When Fairies Come Calling

If it's easier for children who live close to woods, parks and beaches to connect with fairies, what happens to all the children who don't have this luxury? How do they fare? When I caught up with Karen, a graphic designer and busy mum with three children, it was interesting to learn that even when a child's environment isn't ideal, as long as they have access to a tiny pocket of nature, remarkable things can still happen.

Karen remembers the fairies she saw from her bedroom window when she was nine. Though her family home was in a semi-industrial area, they were blessed to have a lovely old garden. 'We lived in an ordinary house with an extraordinary fruit tree garden,' she explains. 'The house was across the road from a railway line, that mainly transported animals to a nearby abattoir. Not the kind of neighbourhood one would expect to find magic!'

*I've spent my life looking for this fairy
magic in people and places.*

Karen lived for the rambling garden, full of apple, peach, plum
and lemon trees. There was even a pecan tree. The tree Karen felt
closest to was a giant mulberry. It had been struck by lightning
years before, leaving one huge branch bent over and spanning
the width of the garden. 'Sitting in the mulberry tree was where
I felt safest,' Karen tells. 'It gave me a real sense of belonging.
I'd sit on the broken branch. The tree felt like my home, like I
could live there and stay there, because I felt it would protect
me. Once a year, I'd climb into the tree with my aunties, and
we'd collect mulberry fruit to make jam.'

The fairies Karen saw visited her over two nights at dusk.
This magical incident took place a couple of years after the family
had moved there. Karen remembers seeing three fairies. 'One
was definitely a roly-poly male fairy,' she recalls. 'The other two,
I'm not sure how to describe them, but they all had wings, no
dresses. They "emerged" onto the branch and were busy going
about their work. The two smaller fairies looked surprised to see
me, because they didn't expect me to be able to see them. After
long moments staring at each other, they backed up and disappeared back into the tree.'

It's intriguing that Karen saw these fairies in a tree, one of
the many gateways to the fairy realm. 'I'd looked out at that tree
a million times,' she reflects, 'but somehow this time, on this
particular night, was the perfect time.'

It's an interesting point Karen makes. It gives us another clue
as to when we are likely to glimpse fairies. We see them when

everything lines up, when we're in balance. In that moment, we're able to slip beyond the stress and busyness of everyday life and experience other worlds. And when those magical moments happen, life is never quite the same again. A tree or flower is no longer just another tree or flower. They're miracles. Or as Karen puts it: 'That moment I saw those little fairies changed my life. I knew I'd witnessed something special, and that from now on I wasn't just dealing with the human world. I suddenly realised there was so much more, that there was magic. I've spent my life looking for this fairy magic again in people and places.'

Looking back, Karen says she spent more time in the garden than in the house. She's convinced her time spent playing in the garden helped her access the fairy realm. Here she delighted in mixing up concoctions of berries and leaves and anything else she could find. Then she would fill the jars with water and these special garden ingredients. 'They watered my garden well,' Karen recollects. 'I made garden beds and a cubby from an old chicken shed. My mother helped. I think she loved this little world as much as I did. She even used to sleep down in that shed on some nights. That special space comforted her too.'

*The moment I saw those little fairies changed my life.
I knew I'd witnessed something special ...
I suddenly realised there was so much
more, that there was magic.*

KAREN

Karen has always had the 'gift of sight'. But as the years went by, she let go her other-worldly gift. 'Then five and a half years ago, it all opened back up. I decided to find out what my purpose was. It's still being revealed to me,' says Karen. 'But my vision is of a planet covered in fruit trees. It's the dream that lies at the very heart of my being. I can see what the earth would look like from the sky, the shades of colour across the land. Can you imagine the kind of magic a world covered with trees would bring?'

Like everyone I spoke with, Karen lives in the real world, working hard as a mum and graphic designer. Yet among the busyness, she's learnt to create pockets of stillness. When she was twenty-five, she left her job as a conference sales manager at a major city hotel to go to the country with her mother, who'd just had a heart attack and needed a change. That was when Karen started writing about her childhood, to gain some perspective on what had happened to her while growing up. Without thinking much about what she was doing, Karen began making collages from old magazines and travel brochures to pass the time and do something creative.

Much to her surprise and delight, Karen suddenly realised she was recreating her childhood garden. Having seen fairies, Karen is left with a determination to embrace all the beauty and wonderment she can. And like so many who have seen fairies, she is always on the lookout for the extraordinary, carefully concealed in those things which at first glance seem ordinary.

Fairy Tasks

When you look at some of the words used in connection with fairies, they give us some clues about these remarkable beings. Fairies are often referred to as 'nature spirits' or 'elementals', as fairies often live and work in nature, and with the building blocks or elements of life. Others talk of fairies as 'the shining ones', given that they are radiant and brimful with life. Others describe fairies as 'the good people' or 'the fair people', as a way of capturing their beauty and benevolent presence in nature. Scottish seer, R J Stewart, talks of fairies as 'our natural allies between the outer realm of manifest nature and the inner realm of ever-becoming, of transformation, of boundless potential.' He also describes them as 'our cousins in the art of perfection and the health of the land and the planet.'[9] How lovely is that?

It's only as I ventured further into the fairy world that I discovered what those who live close to the earth are well aware of—fairies are the living spirit of plants and trees, mountains and deserts, oceans and brooks. They are the invisible presence, the radiant energy found in these and all life forms. Fairies come in countless forms and, like all life forms, they continue to evolve.

Fairies are dazzling to us,
because they are untouched by selfishness or desire.

With so many fairies around, what do they all do? Fairies work tirelessly to nurture and protect nature. It's the fairies who help enrich the soil and assist seeds to germinate. Their loving work enables rivers, valleys and mountain ranges to flourish. Fairies also help with death and decay, so they're an important part of the life cycle. Sometimes you can glimpse these busy nature spirits in tree trunks and flowers, and in dew-drenched spider webs. And whenever you're inspired by a tiny leaf or twig, or a vast mountain range, a nature spirit is reaching out to you, offering you a chance to reconnect with the natural world and with your own inner nature.

People often describe fairies as dazzling, as they're so luminous. It's not hard for fairies to shine, because they're untouched by selfishness or desire. Unlike you or me, they have little experience of suffering, except for what they see in our world. And as they don't get caught up in turbulent emotions, their bodies experience far less wear and tear. That's why, in part, fairies appear ever-young and lovely. This doesn't mean fairies live forever, but they do live much longer than we do. When their lives come to an end, fairies willingly give themselves back to creation, because they love nature so completely.

Fairies do not think of life in terms of
power, so much as service.

The power these little nature spirits have at their fingertips is astonishing. But fairies do not think of life in terms of power, so much as service. Everything they do is for their beloved earth. It is their greatest joy to serve creation. That's why fairies happily give themselves to the plants and trees. There's nothing they would not do for them, because nature is the love of their lives. And though fairies work constantly, they do not grow weary, because they are fed by the love and appreciation that flows from the life form they're taking care of.

When the time comes for a fairy to leave their beloved plant or tree, the life force withdraws and the tree or plant dies. While this is poignant it's not nearly as sad as it sounds, because nothing in the universe ever really dies. It simply changes form.

In-Between Places

Assuming fairies exist, where do you find them? The simple answer is that there are many gateways between worlds, but few are within easy reach. In addition, fairies are very careful about who they let into their world. That's why most gateways to the fairy realms are in unexpected, out-of-the-way places, deliberately hidden from view.

So while you may wish with all your heart to enter the world of fairies, you cannot do so on a whim or by willpower alone. You need to prove yourself worthy, by aligning yourself with the heightened, gossamer-thin energies where fairies operate. You can achieve this in a thousand uplifting ways. By walking more lightly on the earth. By loving and nurturing nature, and being more observant there. By being more outward-looking, less self-absorbed. All these actions will help build your 'light bridge' to the fairies, to enable you to see those things that would otherwise be invisible to you.

Some of the most powerful gateways to the fairy realms are 'in-between' places, so named because they're neither here or there. Many fairy stories hint at where in-between locations can be found, such as in caves, at crossroads and standing stones, as well as springs and wells. In-between places aren't fixed spaces. They have a very fluid quality about them. These places are ever-becoming and filled with endless possibilities. Some people refer to these gateways as 'thin' places, because the veil between our everyday world and that of the fairies is easier to penetrate there. In-between places also have a heightened, more refined energy about them, which again helps open the enchanted doors to the fairy realms.

Fairies are very careful about who they let into their world, because they know just how finely balanced life is. One careless word or action can cause untold harm.

Discovering in-between places is one of the most exciting insights of all things fairy, as these spaces hold huge potential. But how can you recognise an in-between place? When you're in a true threshold or in-between place, you experience a sudden sense of expansion and freedom. Liberated from petty worries, you glimpse your potential and the potential of all things. When you're in the in-between, there's often no sense of time passing. Everything just is. Deliciously promising, in-between places are brimful of unfulfilled possibilities aching to be realised. Looking back, I've no doubt that my experience with the grass coming alive the way it did was because I'd unwittingly slipped into the in-between. Back then, I'd no idea what to do with what was offered to me, other than to be grateful for that luminous moment.

So, what can you do when you find yourself in the in-between? You'll know when you're in an in-between place, as it has a different feel. All your sensations are heightened. Sometimes this is exhilarating. Sometimes it's a little scary, as there's little or nothing familiar to hold onto. Don't panic, if you feel a bit uncomfortable. Discomfort can also be a friend, helping to nudge you out of old unhelpful thoughts and patterns.

It's not every day that we're able to access the in-between, so don't waste a precious opportunity to free yourself from all the things that normally hold you back. When you're in the in-between, your perceptions are opened up way beyond anything you'd normally experience. In this numinous limitless space, past, present and future meet. It's here that your destiny is within reach. Once you get over the unsettling sense of being swept far away from everything that's familiar, a new feeling emerges. You begin to feel as if anything is possible, which it is. So don't downplay or dismiss this expansive moment. Stay anchored in who you are and what your soul seeks most—renewed joy, more courage, less pain—whatever matters deeply to you. Then open yourself up to the possibility that these qualities can be yours here and now.

When you're in an in-between place and you become still, it's a good idea to ask that you only draw in energies and experiences that are for your highest good. Then try to get a real feel of the place. Notice how your uncertainty sharpens your impressions. Everything is far more vivid than usual, which is wonderful but can also be distracting. Stay calm and centred, so your true 'sight' has room to emerge amid the heightening of your senses. All at once, you'll find yourself able to think and see further than normal. Wonderfully creative ideas or solutions to difficult situations may present themselves in lightning flashes of insight.

Frequently, these insights will be left field, because the in-between draws on the universe's limitless wisdom and creative potential.

It helps to prepare yourself for in-between moments, by aligning yourself to the refined energy you may encounter there. You can achieve this by spending time in sacred and/or beautiful locations, places that lift your life energy, which in turn helps bring you closer to the delicate light-filled world of the fairies. What happens then is a meeting and expansion of light. Your radiance touches that of fairy folk, and in doing so creates new possibilities for us all. You can grow your radiance through meditation and prayer. Through a commitment to peace. A life of kindness. Through a genuine love of creation.

But a word of caution here. Be careful what you wish for. Be very clear about what you are seeking while in the in-between, so you can recognise what is true and what is not. A lack of preparation can leave you vulnerable, can have you chasing glittering possibilities that feed your ego but have little true substance. When you're unable to discern what it is your soul needs, you're likely to go off on tangents, grasping at things that turn out to be illusory or dissolve into ashes before you.

As your everyday sight shuts down,
you begin to experience other ways of seeing and being.

There are countless places where we can step into the in-between. Drawn to all things Celtic, my soul soars whenever the mist enfolds me. I love the subtlety and power of this in-between place. Sensual, calming and spellbinding, the mist causes the everyday world to recede, allowing more of life's secrets to reveal themselves. When I can only see a few steps in front of me, something within expands and I start to experience other ways of seeing and being. This doesn't mean I let go of all caution in the mist, as in all in-between places. For as tantalising and brimful of possibilities as mist is, it's essential that amid my wonderment I don't lose track of my true self—who I am at my essence and what truly fills my soul. Otherwise, it would be all too easy to lose myself in the midst of all the excitement and welter of possibilities, then my ego could take over and become caught up in the power and seeming glamour of the moment. So, as mesmerising as the in-between is, it's essential to move forward slowly and carefully. Then, as the silence enfolds us, we begin to see ourself and the world in a new light.

There are also in-between times of day that can help you access the fairy realms. Dawn is a very powerful in-between time. As the world is caressed by the first rays of the sun, everything shimmers with fresh potential. Brimful with life, dawn offers many gifts. That's why, in times past, people harvested plants and herbs at the start of the day. That's why it's good to rise with the sun and embrace all the good a new day offers.

Sunset is another in-between time. At the end of the day, when the shadows deepen and the sunlight casts a warm glow over the land, all kinds of enchanting opportunities await you. As the world softens and its colours fade, many tiny details that pass you by during the day become apparent. In this enchanted space between day and night, new possibilities beckon, as all that's familiar fades away into darkness.

If you look carefully, you'll discover these transition places all around you. Fairies love life's in-between places, because they understand the immense promise they hold. The life energy is strong there, helping fairies stay ever-young, ever-becoming. When you're in an in-between place, you're poised between your doubts and dreams, between hope and fear. In these most magical of moments, you have the chance to find a new way of walking in the world. To be wiser and more inspired. More at peace. More willing to follow what you know in your heart to be true.

If special work is needed or you want to create something out of the ordinary, to mend the past or envision a new future, seek out an in-between place. Then, with the help of the fairies, allow your new dreams to take shape.

Fairies do not question your right to free will,
but gently point out that free will is
not the same thing as freedom.
Free will can imprison you or liberate you.
So the fairies suggest you choose
whatever you seek carefully.

The Miracle of Trees

So where else might you encounter fairies? Believe it or not, trees are also gateways to the fairy realms. If you read Enid Blyton's *The Magic Faraway Tree*[10] as a child, you'll remember the many adventures Jo, Fanny and Bessie shared on venturing up the magic faraway tree and accessing other worlds there. This gripping children's story, which captured the imagination of millions, touches on something quite profound. As trees are in-between places, they help you access other worlds. Moreover, every tree has its own fairy caretaker, who lovingly protects and cares for the tree for the term of its natural life. Some fairies remain with their assigned tree for centuries. Others will only be with their tree for a handful of years. When a tree fairy finally withdraws from its beloved tree, the tree's life energy fades and the tree dies.

When you approach trees with genuine love in your heart,
You'll never walk the world as a stranger.

When I first started to explore all things fairy, these and other insights seemed a bit far-fetched. Yet as I mulled over these possibilities, I realised there is something very special about trees, old trees in particular. This is apparent in the extraordinary photos exceptional photographers take of ancient trees. We also get a sense of the powerful presence of trees in the mesmerisingly beautiful illustrations of gnarled trees found in children's storybooks.

I'd always assumed the strange faces and unusual figures seen in intricate illustrations of tree trunks were a product of the artist's vivid imagination, until I met British healer and teacher, Lorna Todd. One day while out walking with Lorna, I began to really see the nature spirits in trees for myself. Lorna literally opened a window on a world I knew little about, but had sensed for some time. I'm eternally grateful for the many wise observations Lorna shared about trees and their resident fairies, and for enabling me to glimpse these enchanting beings.

When you connect deeply with a tree, sooner or later its fairy caretaker will reveal itself. You may see the tree spirit, or experience a sudden electric or uplifting sensation. You may be aware of the sudden stirring of a breeze when everything else is still. However the connection happens, it will touch your heart deeply, sparking an immediate recognition that something significent is taking place. Becoming one with the spirit of a tree is such a sacred experience. It reconnects you to the web of life, to the deep magic of existence underpinning the living world. This may seem light years from where you are currently at, but rest assured that if I'm able to connect with fairy tree spirits, you can too.

A good way to connect with tree fairy spirits is to foster a relationship with trees of all kinds. You might like to start by simply finding a tree you're drawn to. Once you've located that tree, get to know its unique shape, feel and scent. Study its bark. Allow your eyes to follow the shape and direction of its boughs. See how the tree reaches up to embrace the sky. Take note of how it clothes itself in summer. Delight in its autumnal grandeur. Savour the stark beauty of its bare limbs, as winter closes in. Then as you get to know the tree, you'll find a subtle communication starts to develop between you. Little by little, you'll begin to sense the tree's different moods. This isn't a relationship to be hurried so much as enjoyed. Don't be tempted to rush things. Allow the relationship to unfold over days and weeks. Make sure that your touch is always loving and your motives pure, then who knows what special moments may await you? The tree fairy may just smile on you. If and when you do make contact with a tree fairy, you're accessing the essence of the tree.

While this all sounds very lovely, until you've made your own connection this may possibly seem a little unreal. So let's take a closer look at the ways in which trees are gateways to the fairy kingdom.

Several decades ago, Scottish scientist and mystic Robert Ogilvie Crombie (Roc), had his first fairy encounter while sitting under his favourite beech tree in Edinburgh's Royal Botanic Garden. Roc was simply out in the fresh air enjoying the afternoon. He was leaning against a beech tree that he really loved, when he suddenly became very aware of the tree and everything about it, from the tree's sap to its roots. The experience was so vivid that Roc felt as if he were the tree. At the same moment, he felt a sudden heightening of his awareness. Then, to his surprise, he saw a tiny faun about three feet high, dancing around on the lawn.

Trained in chemistry, maths and physics, Roc wasn't given to flights of fancy, so at first assumed the faun was a boy in fancy dress. But as he watched the figure more intently, he realised this wasn't the case. When this intriguing little stranger discovered that Roc could see him, he was just as surprised, as most humans no longer see fairies. This lovely little faun explained to Roc that he lived in the botanical gardens, and that his job was to help the trees grow. He ended up talking with Roc for some time and promised he would see Roc again, as long as Roc summoned him.[11]

Roc's first fairy encounter holds many insights. You begin to sense just how much of a bridge to the fairy realms trees can be. Roc was relaxing under a tree he had a special relationship with, when he saw the fairy. This incident only happened after Roc's awareness was lifted to a new level. In this moment of heightened awareness, Roc became one with the tree. From his description, it sounds like this was a truly ecstatic moment. As his whole being was elevated and expanded, Roc made the energetic leap from our world of matter to that of the fairy, without even realising what was happening. Then the fairy faun appeared to him without any effort. Everyone's experience of fairies will be different, but Roc's account reveals a great deal about how contact with fairies takes place.

A tree also played a central role in Renee's first fairy encounter. This young city-based graphic artist saw her fairies on a tree outside her apartment. 'I used to live on the top floor of an apartment block, and there was this big tree outside my window,' she tells. 'One evening, I saw all these blue fairies in the tree. It was twilight. Then I started to see fairies regularly. The feeling with these blue fairies was that they were like little guardians. They all had their jobs with plants and trees and things. They were actually quite territorial, like birds. It's like they were saying, "This is my tree. I look after this tree".' Renee has no doubt that having a loving relationship with the tree outside her apartment enabled her to see the fairies. Now she regularly sees fairies in a whole range of locations. She even saw fairies one day while giving a client presentation.

There were all these little beings around me giggling. They were about knee height. There were so many of them.

DESPINA

Trees were also a doorway to the world of fairies for Despina, a busy young sales manager. Though she'd always loved trees, it wasn't until her twenties that Despina encountered fairies in one particular tree. She was staying with Susan, a healer friend who lived in a canyon near Malibu. 'Susan's very down to earth and grounded. She showed me around the property with her dog. It's a massive, massive property,' Despina recollects. 'There were lots of trees and I love them, so I felt very excited and peaceful there. The weather was beautiful. As I was walking around, there was one particular tree I was drawn to. It had overhanging branches and you could walk underneath them. The child in me was excited by the thought of walking under the tree, but another part of me wasn't so sure. When I walked under the tree, all of a sudden I could feel a more lovely energy around me. There were all these little beings around me, giggling. They were about knee height. There were so many of them.

'It was so obvious the fairies were there. There was lots of joy. It was like they were waiting for me. They were excited for me. They had lots of different personalities. Some were gnome-like. Others were more feminine, and had a more transparent, lighter energy. Then I began to wonder what was going on. Was there really something there, or was I losing my mind? When I asked Susan if I was imagining it, she said no. She asked me what I thought it was. I said, "I think there's fairy kind of dudes around here" and she agreed. She left me with the fairies. I was totally in awe. I was standing looking around at them. There were like rays of sunlight going through the fairies and lighting up different patches. It was another world, like in the storybooks.' As Despina shared this special moment with me over coffee, there was a real sense of reverence in her recollections. It took us both way beyond the excitement of Despina having connected with fairies, to a space that felt truly sacred. What I've come to realise is that such fairy experiences help connect us to ourselves, to nature, to the divine in all things.

There were like rays of sunlight going through
the fairies and lighting up different patches.
It was another world, like in the storybooks.

DESPINA

Shortly afterwards, I came across Erika through a special writer friend. Erika's first contact with fairies took place in a forest. Based in Switzerland, Erika has worked in banking most of her life. Erika was in the middle of a clairvoyance course when Evelyne, one of her teachers, offered to take them on a field trip into the forest. Once everyone was in the woods, Evelyne invited them to find a space they were drawn to and sit down, then wait quietly to see what happened. 'I walked around a bit because I couldn't decide where to sit, then finally chose a little moss-covered place next to a moss-covered tree,' Erika tells. 'It was a little bit away from all the others.' Settling down, she began to worry about what she was doing there, and whether she was likely to see anything.

'After a while I was feeling a little bit bored, so I just decided to wait quietly for the end of the exercise. I started to examine the moss at my feet, and suddenly thought I saw it moving up and down, like it was breathing. That made me wonder if I was crazy, but as there was nothing else to do, I just continued to look at the moss. After a few seconds, a lovely girl fairy appeared. She was about four inches high, smiling and dancing happily among the moss. She was wearing a blue dress with a ribbon around her waist, and was holding a marguerite flower in her hand as an umbrella. The fairy was barefoot and not taking any notice of me. Then I realised she was not on her own. A boy fairy followed her, dancing, laughing and whistling. He was barefoot too, and not taking any notice of me either. He wore a daisy on his head like a hat, and he had his hands in the pockets of his three-quarter trousers. The third fairy I saw was another girl fairy, and she wore a skirt too. She had some little flowers in her hair and ran after the others. It was so cute! I saw all this right next to me, right next to my feet! I thought I was fantasising, waking from a nice dream, so I shook my head then looked up and the fairies were gone.'

Remarkably, Erika had more fairy experiences on that same outing. 'Ten or twenty yards away I saw other nature spirits,' she tells. 'They looked scary, compared with the nice little fairies I'd just seen. These fairies had long pointed ears, prominent noses, long hair and wore hats. They were maybe three or so feet high. For some reason, they reminded me of Robin Hood. They behaved completely differently to the first group of fairies. To this day, I can't tell you whether I saw one nature spirit several times, or several different nature spirits. Either way, they were able to beam themselves to another place within a fraction of a second!

'They hid behind different trees. One by one, they stepped out of the shadow of the tree for a brief moment, made funny faces at me, like putting their two index fingers in the corners of their mouth, pulling at each side of their mouth and sticking their tongue out, then quickly hid behind the tree again. Another put his two thumbs on the side of his head, waved his fingers and stuck out his tongue. Yet another scratched his armpits, dancing, laughing and hopping around. He giggled and made funny noises, then quickly hid behind the tree. Again I thought I was dreaming, so I shook my head and the nature spirits were gone. The second experience was less enjoyable, but funny nevertheless. As I look back today, I think the second group of fairies wanted me to ginger up. They were making me laugh again, because I was really lovesick at that time.'

The joyful mischief of Erica's fairies shines through her account. It's fascinating to discover this lighthearted approach helped Erika get over the heartache she was experiencing at the time.

The greater your affinity with trees and their fairy caretakers, the more you will start to connect with nature in the most beautiful and unexpected ways. 'In the last five years, I have been more accepting of my awareness or sensitivity to the environment around me,' admits Karen, a busy mum and graphic artist. 'I can feel tree spirits. There's a communication there I can open up to. About eight weeks ago, my beautiful jambu tree in our garden told me that if I planted mango trees in the yard, they would be growing mature fruit in five years. I was hanging out the washing at the time. The funny thing was, I was thinking about planting mango trees just before this, and then out of nowhere this tree tells me what to do.'

This contact with fairies is real and can be life-changing. But how can you build a deeper relationship with trees and their fairy caretakers? After getting to know a tree, it's important to listen to what it has to say. Try not to be too impatient for something to happen. Simply start to get a sense of how the fairy spirit of the tree would like to talk to you. It may be through the creaking of the tree's boughs, or the soft rustle of its leaves, or the way the tree sways in the wind. Once you start to notice what's happening with the tree, you'll be surprised by how much it has to share.

Connecting with trees and their fairy caretakers isn't something that's only available to those living in rural areas, as city-based artist Roshilla discovered. 'Trees have their own magic, and every one is unique. They're so powerful,' she tells. 'The first time I saw a tree spirit, I saw a hand coming out of the tree giving light to the world, so I painted it. I also noticed that one tree outside my house has roots that look like hands going down deep into the earth. It was so beautiful. Then late last year, I was going for a walk and there was no wind. I was lost in my thoughts at the time. Something made me turn round, and all I could see were these two tiny branches waving at me. Like they were really waving, while everything else was still. There was no-one else around. I just burst into laughter. Trees are brilliant. They bring me into the present moment. I don't know what I'd do without them.'

Trees have their own magic, and every one is so unique. They're so powerful.

ROSHILLA

Trees and their fairy keepers willingly nurture people and help them keep going, even when life seems impossibly hard. Sadly, too few of us realise what's going on. 'I've always had an affinity with trees,' explains Despina, now in her thirties. 'Growing up in the city, I didn't have trees around me that much. But when I was a child we lived near a river and there were a lot of trees there. When I was eleven it was a really hot summer, so we used to go to the park straight from school. It was really dry. Fire weather. I always remember the trees there, the feel and smell of them. I had a sense of belonging with the trees, which was a real lifesaver, as everything else around me was a bit manic. As a girl, I didn't feel very safe in the world, not good enough, very separated from other people. I felt a bit different, a bit shy. But I felt a real contentment with trees. It was like they were more my family. The trees gave me a sense of belonging and safety, like I was okay. Every time I go back to that park as an adult, the same comforting feelings come up.'

I felt a real contentment with trees. It was
like they were more my family.
The trees gave me a sense of belonging
and safety, like I was okay.

DESPINA

Swiss-born Celia, now in her nineties, cannot imagine her childhood without one special tree in the garden, which inspired and comforted her. 'The tall apple tree in my garden felt like a kind of mother to me,' she recalls. 'It was my shelter and my very own home, not to be shared with anyone else. My mother had died when I was just one year old. In our early childhood, none of our several nannies or housekeepers could ever form a meaningful bond with my brother or myself. The apple tree's angel-like being emanated a caring motherly feeling, which touched me deeply as a young child. The shape of its branches offered lots of opportunities for imaginary games. So there was a dining room, a kitchen with a hole in the trunk, serving as a ready-made cooking pot. There was also a reading room where my books, once I could read, were supported by a branch. The highest enjoyment was in "my" bedroom, where I could lie for what seemed hours, staring up at the sky through the pattern of foliage and twigs.'

Trees bring such comfort that it can be devastating for children when they no longer have access to them, as Celia discovered. 'I cried bitter tears and felt shocked and inconsolable, on coming home from school one day to see the tree had been cut down,' she tells. 'Although I was in first year of high school, the unexpectedness of seeing my beloved apple tree lying there on the grass hacked into pieces still stays in my memory, as clearly as if it were yesterday. It was almost unbearable. The tree, I was told in a matter of fact voice, had to make way for a new road.'

Whether you live in a small town or big city, never underestimate what trees and their fairy caretakers can bring to your life. For Sarah, a young manager with a busy job, trees have been a lifesaver. 'When you're deeply centred in yourself without thought or anything, you can get on the same level as a tree,' she explains. 'If you really feel into that tree, you discover it has stories to tell. For me, trees and their fairies talk through feelings. I get information from them through these feelings, and also insights to help me with my life.'

The close relationship that people like Sarah, Celia, Despina, Roshilla and Roc enjoy with trees is nothing new. For generations, people have sought out trees for inspiration and protection, for solace and shade. Children seem to understand that there's something special about trees, without having to be told. Left to their own devices, they'll climb up into a tree, or simply lie on a branch and stare up at the sky. When you look back at your own childhood, perhaps there were trees where you'd hide or daydream, where you played for hours on end? And did you retreat to certain trees when life became too much? Whenever you connect with a tree, you're also connecting to its fairy spirit.

Trees constantly give of their abundance,
but rarely do we acknowledge them and their fairy caretakers.

Trees and their fairy keepers are woven into our lives in all kinds of unexpected ways. Annette, who was involved in migrant education, discovered that leaving behind the tree they'd grown up with was one of the hardest things for refugees abandoning their homes and countries. Many of them felt this loss keenly.

Trees are also the lungs of our planet, supporting countless life forms. They constantly give of their abundance, but rarely do we think about what trees and their resident fairies do for us. Our lives are so full on, it's often hard to imagine things could be any other way. So even though you may not have a relationship with trees right now, it's never too late to get to know the trees around you, and to encourage your children to do the same. Why not take a walk in the woods instead of to the movies or shopping mall? Who knows what enchanted moments may await you?

Talking Trees

The astonishing thing is that trees not only nourish and inspire us, they communicate with us as well. While this may seem a little way out, talking with trees isn't exactly a new concept. Fairy tales are full of trees that have plenty to say. When you're open to this possibility, it's more likely to happen for you.

Linda, a busy New Zealand executive, had never given this much thought until a tree in her garden spoke out. 'We lived in the inner city on the corner of a busy road,' she tells. 'This road didn't worry us at all, as we had the most beautiful oak tree that stood as a sentinel for us in our garden. It gave us privacy and something of nature to look at. I would lie in bed and watch this tree over the seasons. It was always a beautiful sight. There was an ivy creeper that took up more and more of the garden over time. Then it started to move up the trunk of our tree. I didn't like to spray the ivy, so I went out one day with my small kitchen knife to cut the creeper off the trunk. In a moment of inattention the knife slipped, and the blade entered the tree. There was a terrible noise, something I cannot really describe. It made me think there'd been an accident on the road, so I jumped up and looked out over the fence, only to find the road was deserted. It was then I realised it was the tree that had made the noise. It was the sound of pain. You can imagine how much apologising I did!'

Some trees have stood for hundreds of years
and have witnessed many things.
That's why they're so wise.
The older the tree, the more wisdom it
accumulates, the more wisdom it has to share.

In getting to know trees, I've come to appreciate how much they respond to what's going on around them. A couple of years ago, an unusual incident gave me a real sense of how much trees and their resident fairies take in. I was giving an early evening talk at a city bookstore. My back was to the bookshop's front window, which looked out onto a street full of traffic and passers-by. As I was speaking, I noticed an older lady gazing out of the window with a wonderful smile on her face. She seemed to be totally at peace. When I'd finished, she came up to me and said she wished I'd been sitting where she was, because every time I talked about nature, the aura of the tree outside the shop window filled with bright swirls of beautiful colours. I was amazed to think that, despite all the noise and traffic on the busy street, the tree could pick up on what was being talked about inside the bookstore. I've thought about that incident often in quiet moments. It's left me wondering how trees cope with the crush of people and pollution in our cities, given that they're so sensitive.

Life in our frenetic world can be difficult for trees and their fairy spirits. Yet in spite of this, trees are immensely patient. Some trees have stood for hundreds of years and have witnessed many things. That's why they're so wise. The older the tree, the more wisdom it accumulates, and the more wisdom it has to share. So when a tree is cut down, much is lost. It's desperately sad when a tree has its natural cycle cut short, because trees are not only part of the delicate balance of life, they're wisdom-keepers too.

As your relationship with trees and their fairy caretakers deepens, you'll find that being around trees is a bit like falling in love. You just can't get enough of them. 'Trees are living beings with feelings,' says Susan, a busy mum, teacher and artist. 'To me they're like people. I have this deep love for them. When I walk past a tree, it feels like a person to me. I love to hug and be with trees. I feel a deep love for them. I love them a lot.'

The older the tree, the more wisdom it accumulates.
And so when a tree is cut down, much is lost.

If you allow the love between you and a tree that captures your attention to blossom, you'll find the love just keeps on growing. 'I put my hands on all the trees I can; I do it all the time,' admits sales manager Despina. 'For me, it's the same as putting my hand on someone's back, like greeting an old friend. I do it with all the trees I come across. Some really speak to me.' As with any relationship, the closer you get to a tree, the more it reveals. 'When I'm really connected to a tree, all the barriers dissolve,' explains Despina. 'I feel like I can walk straight through trees, like they're gel-like, like I can merge with them. This happens particularly when I've been on a vision quest and have leant up against a tree for 24 hours.'

It's strange that we're only just starting to discover what the ancients knew well: trees and their fairy caretakers are also keepers of a great deal of wisdom. Many trees are willing to share what they've learnt, if you take the time to listen. After a trip to Egypt and Greece, Despina ended her holiday with a trip to Delphi, where the famous oracle of old was situated. When the tour arrived at Delphi, everyone piled out of the bus and started heading up the track. Despina got partway up the track, when she felt one particular tree calling her. As she already had a close relationship with trees, Despina didn't hesitate to sit by the tree to see what might happen. She describes her time with this tree as 'like being in the presence of a teacher'. One of the reasons she had gone on this holiday was to get greater clarity about her life and what to do next. As Despina listened to what the tree told her, she was shown the best way forward. She was so moved that the tree spirit had reached out to her, had answered all the questions she'd been wrestling with, and helped recharge her batteries. After that brief encounter, Despina had such clarity she was ready to go home and get on with life.

Bev also told of how much she learnt from one of the trees in her garden. 'One day I was out hugging my peppercorn tree on a really blustery day, when it said to me, "Don't flap around wildly. Stay calm and centred, and bend with the wind." When I looked round, I saw how the other trees were being buffeted about and creating a lot of noise. But when I looked at the peppercorn tree, it was swaying gently.' Over time, Bev developed a special relationship with her peppercorn tree. She's now able to communicate with it and learn many things. 'This tree has my "fairy" bell on it,' she tells. 'Even if it is quite breezy the bell does not ring. It only rings at unexpected times.'

The great Chief Walking Buffalo of Canada's Stoney Indians talks beautifully about what trees can bring to our lives: 'I have learnt a lot from trees. Something about the weather, something about animals, and something about the Great Spirit.' This deeper relationship with trees and their fairy keepers is something we can all enjoy. It's not about superstition, but rather learning to live alongside the rest of creation with love and respect, and about being prepared to listen and learn. When we do, remarkable things happen.

More than once a tree, or in this case a giant cactus, has shared its wisdom with me, and it's always what I needed to hear. Some years back I was in the Sonoran Desert in Arizona, marvelling at the huge saguaro cacti often seen in Westerns. Over a couple of hundred years, these cacti can grow to up to 150 feet high and weigh up to 4 tonnes. Staring in awe at one particular majestic cactus, I felt as if I were standing before a great elder, whose arms were raised above me in a silent blessing.

Not wanting to waste this special moment, I asked the spirit of this saguaro to please give me some guidance for my path ahead. Without hesitation it responded, telling of the importance of boundaries, and pointing out that if it didn't have spikes it would never survive. 'Saguaro don't set out to hurt other creatures with their spikes, but we do need them to protect ourselves,' it explained. 'We all have a right to our boundaries, and when our boundaries are honoured, no-one is disadvantaged.'

As I stood in 100°F heat, the saguaro went on to talk about the absolute importance of conserving our life energy. It explained to me that until the rains come in summer months, the saguaro exist in a bone-dry environment, often in gruelling temperatures. 'If we were to waste our resources at such times we would die,' it told me. 'So we hold our resources close until the time is right, then we act, so nothing is lost.'

This saguaro spoke about life in ways I'd never fully understood. 'The web of life is not just about connection with the rest of life, it's about support,' it said. 'When we genuinely belong to the whole of life, we can relax and allow other forms of creation to help support us, instead of doing everything alone. It's a far more fulfilling way to live.' This was such a powerful insight for me, and I suspect for all of us.

As this remarkable cactus continued to thrive in unforgiving terrain, I realised it had so much to teach about the nuances of life. Were I able to spent a few days or weeks there, I'm sure I could have filled whole books with the wisdom it so generously offered. As I left the desert that day, my heart was full as I pondered the many insights that giant saguaro cactus gave me— insights I very much needed to hear.

Such incidents allow us to glimpse just how close a relationship we can enjoy with nature and its fairy caretakers. When you're prepared to reconnect with the living world, it brings you back to a profound relationship with yourself and with the whole of creation. You start to access ever-deepening insights into life and your life's purpose. Never again will you feel that terrifying sense of isolation, because you'll know who you are and where you belong.

THE ANCIENT FAERY TRADITION …. IS NOT A
RELIGION, IT'S A WAY OF RELATING.[12]

R J Stewart

When Nature Reaches Out to You

My fairy discoveries didn't end with trees. As I delved into the importance of trees in the cosmos, I began to realise trees are not our only connecting point in nature with fairies. Slowly, I began to see that whenever we're drawn to a rock or stone, or the sweet tumble of water in a mountain stream, the fairies are there also. It's simply yet another way of trying to get your attention. Fairies often communicate with you through your senses. Through an achingly lovely flower, an intoxicating perfume, or the astonishing display of colours splashed across the sky at sunset.

So when something inside you sings to experience the bliss of a balmy summer's night, to see the first signs of spring after a long winter, or to savour the deep silence that descends after a fresh fall of snow, the fairies are reaching out to you, offering you the chance to immerse yourself in life's glimmering beauty, to feel fully alive. If you pay attention to these moments, you'll know that the next time you long to feel the soft tickle of grass beneath your feet, or experience the bite of the summer sun on your arms and face, these invitations are precious and beneficial, because they're invitations to fill yourself with life.

> *Whenever you ache to connect with nature,*
> *know the fairies are offering you the*
> *chance to replenish, to be inspired,*
> *to get clear about yourself and your life,*
> *to enjoy more peace and beauty.*

Fairies love to help you back into balance, because when you're more whole, the world is too. You can help this process along by actively embracing the beauty around you. So absorb all the beauty you can in nature. Be grateful for all this loveliness. Allow it to inspire and heal you. Once you begin to experience this new way of relating to the living world, everything around you will begin to change. You will see possibilities where before there were none. You will be drawn to simplicity, to those things which feed the soul. Then when next you drink in the intense green of a meadow, the rich black of the soil or the burnt ochre of ancient rocks, know how much the colours and textures of those landscapes can feed your body and spirit.

The fairies love to speak to you through your senses, so take note of your feelings whenever you're in nature. Do this and you will gain a far more complete understanding of the natural world. I heard recently of a sixteen-year-old girl who'd lost her mother. After her mother died, all this bewildered teenage girl wanted was to be in nature, so she joined a community garden. The girl's instincts served her well. Slowly, she was able to let her terrible grief go, as she worked with the plants and soil.

Bev is also grateful she followed her instincts to get out into nature, after an overwhelming personal loss. 'During my time of grieving, I would go outside and sit on the grass or lie down there,' she tells. 'This was very unusual for me, as I wouldn't even walk on the grass without shoes before that time. I found I needed to lie down and pour my grief into Mother Earth. She accepted my tears, and nurtured and comforted me as I let go of this grief. I would find comfort from her warmth and protection during those times. It has been a tremendous gift.' Looking back, Bev is aware of just how much the earth helped heal her sorrow, and that it was the fairies who helped make this possible.

Frequently, fairies speak to us through our longings. Some of our longings may even surprise us. When Karen was pregnant with her first child, she craved rich damp soil. 'I remember driving along the motorway and seeing huge mounds of clean, glistening soil piled up on the side of the road, and my mouth literally watered,' she recalls. 'I craved soil for the next month or so, and imagined eating it, chewing it.' Karen is the first to admit this was all a bit strange, but now realises she was craving a much deeper connection to the earth.

Bridgette is a young writer and archaeologist based in Buffalo NY. It was her longing to be with the trees near her childhood home, which helped her get over a difficult relocation back to her country of birth. 'I needed to regroup when I returned to America after living in Australia,' she admits. 'I was in Australia for over six years. There's no real seasonal change there. I knew it was time to move on, but part of me was sad to go. When I first moved back home to the States it was autumn, and it was so healing to be back in the deciduous forests with the trees. I get a lot of energy from trees. Being with trees brings me in touch with the spirit of who I am.'

On another occasion, she saw the effect trees and their fairy keepers had on fellow archaeologists. 'I was on a dig somewhere in Kentucky, and we were in this very lovely spot,' Bridgette tells. 'People were talking over lunch. After a while they stopped talking, and just sat there enjoying the peacefulness. No-one spoke. It was a really beautiful wooded location, overlooking more forest. I actually saw the trees send out this peaceful energy and embrace the whole group. It was the most beautiful thing. Just before it happened, I was told to watch out for it. After that, everyone started to go on about how really beautiful the trees were in this location. Here we all were, different kinds of people, but we all felt it. It was like this big hug. I know trees give off negative ions. But it doesn't matter what the physics are, it's like ... experience the gift of it fully.'

Whenever you ache to connect with nature,
the fairies are offering you the chance
to replenish, to be inspired,
to get clear about yourself and your life,
to enjoy more peace and beauty.

Sometimes Bridgette finds she just has to get out into nature. 'I was with friends drinking wine and doing whatever. Suddenly I thought, I really need a dig; I need to have my hands in the dirt and be dirty for a day, and be in the woods and have the earth cleanse me.' It turned out my friend was thinking the same thing. For me, going on a dig isn't so much about the money, and sometimes it's not even about the objects. For me, it's like being in the land, having the dirt on me. I find it's more cleansing than going for a swim.'

Fairies speak to you through your yearnings, because the things you truly long for are significant, and can be transforming. So don't ignore a sudden need to be out in the fresh air or to get away to the country for a weekend. Or perhaps you're drawn to spending some time in the mountains or woods. Whatever your yearnings, the spirit of a place is calling out to you, so pay attention.

Several years ago, I dreamt of leaving the city and journeying deep into the desert. When I woke the following morning, the whole idea seemed crazy. Yet something kept tugging at my sleeve. Months later, I got the chance to visit America's great south-western desert, taking in Colorado, Utah, Arizona and New Mexico. That trip changed my life. Being out in those vast desert landscapes liberated me. Miracle upon miracle followed, because for once I had time and space in my life for deeper things.

We all get invitations to reconnect with nature; the question is what to do about them. Whenever you ache to be in nature, the fairies are offering you the chance to replenish, to be inspired, to get clear about yourself and your life, and to enjoy more peace and beauty. So don't hold back!

The Secrets of Rocks and Stones

As I delved still deeper into the world of nature and her fairy caretakers, I began to look more closely at rocks, stones and pebbles, where I was amazed to discover even more of nature's secrets. I started to see how rocks and stones sit silently among us, preciously guarding the memories of people and events long gone. Over time, I came to realise these ancient record-keepers remember everything they have seen and experienced through time. Now and then they overcome their intense shyness to try to talk to us, but sadly their gentle whispers are often lost on the wind.

So how can you and I restore the sacred connection we once had with rocks and stones, with tiny pebbles and their fairy keepers? Again, it's about reaching out to these beings in love, as rocks and stones respond best to a loving eye and touch. So take a little time to appreciate these opportunities. Don't hesitate to run your hands over a small pebble or vast piece of rock. Take time to observe their unique qualities. As your relationship develops, a whole world of wisdom and beauty will be there for you, and the resident fairy spirit of that rock or stone may also tell you a little of what they know.

Rocks and stones sit silently among us, preciously guarding their memories of people and events long gone.

Celia, now in her nineties, was amazed by her experiences with rocks. 'Many rocks show recognisable shapes, which allow our imagination to get in touch with their essential being,' she explains. 'There is a giant rock near the Porcupine Range where I liked to go walking, which has a clearly visible face. It's half-turned towards where people walk along the track, and half overlooks the steep stony walls of the range. In communicating with the rock, I discovered his task is to hold back the whole mountainside, to stop it from tumbling into the valley. When I pointed this special rock out to my friends, they responded laughingly, saying it was all in my mind! Yet I felt exhilarated by his presence. I could sense the enormous strength he had gained, to help him with his important task of protecting the other rocks and the valley below. We became friends and each time I visited this terrain, his face stood out more and more clearly for me.

'On one of our outings, my friends decided not to accompany me on a further track, so we parted for a while. They waited for me with the picnic. When I returned from my walk, my friends had gone. I looked around, but I could not see them anywhere, so I approached my giant rock friend. He told me with some amusement that my friends were sitting right round on the other side of him. Relieved, I climbed over to a narrow grassy ledge that we had never visited before. Sure enough, there were my friends admiring the magnificent view!'

This level of connection with rocks and stones and their fairy caretakers can only happen when you let go of your notions about what's possible and how things should turn out, and instead see the living world in all its beauty and enchantment.

Rocks are shy. They much prefer to sleep in the ground, but are happy to be placed in a more exposed position, if it is for a sacred purpose.

Some time ago I met Ivan McBeth, a Druid who built standing stones around the world. Some of these mighty stones weighed up to twenty tonnes. Described by Ivan as ancient technology, standing stones are positioned in carefully chosen places on the land to enhance the life there. Early on in his work building standing stones, Ivan and his team were having great difficulty getting one giant stone to move along the wooden rollers used to position them. One of the group suggested they talk to the rock and explain their sacred purpose, in the hope they might enlist its help in moving it into its final position. This seemed like a good idea, so they told the rock their plans and respectfully asked for its help. To their surprise, the rock then slid down the wooden rollers and into its upright position without effort. Once the fairy spirit of that giant rock understood what Ivan and his team were trying to achieve, it was more than happy to cooperate.

Over the years, Ivan came to appreciate how shy rocks were, and how they much preferred to sleep in the ground. The miracle is that standing stones are willing to be in a more exposed position, if it's for a sacred purpose. How beautiful is that?

When you spend time with rocks and stones, you can't help but see them differently. Despina found her relationship with rocks has changed dramatically, since she started to notice them. 'I can look at a rock and I can see the life in it,' she tells. 'When I see it, it's so alive that it's like I could almost get up and walk right through it.'

Phil, who has gone on night walks in nature with mystic and ranger Bob Crombie, has also had some wonderful experiences with what he describes as 'soft rocks'. When Phil walked on these rocks he says they didn't feel like rocks at all. Bob is also familiar with these rocks, and loves being around them. 'They're right out on the edge of the cliffs, where you get a panoramic view south in the daytime,' he tells. 'When I take people there they say that these are great rocks to play on. When you walk on a normal rock it's solid and it jars, but these rocks are very appealing because they're soft. They're part of a whole group of rocks and there's nothing to distinguish one from another. But when you walk on them, you're in a totally different place. It really does feel as if you're walking on something soft.'

There's one particular rock I visit that
I've had different reactions to.
It's lovely to 'paddle' on its back. It feels like childhood joy.
You just want to lie down on it and cuddle it.

Janet

Artist, teacher and busy mum, Janet Selby, has also spent time with these 'soft' rocks. She describes walking on them as being similar to how she felt after an acupuncture session. 'When I walked down the stairs it felt like I had a two-inch layer of sponge on my feet,' she explains. 'That's what it feels like on the soft rock. It feels cushiony. And when you lie down on the rock and enjoy its qualities, it feels very nurturing, even though the rock is sandstone. It helps bring you back into equilibrium.'

Janet's sensitivity around rocks began when she was very young. She suspects that with one rock she got to know as a young girl, she may have inadvertently tapped into its memory of times long gone. 'Whenever I was around this rock, I used to imagine there was an Aboriginal gathering to sing and dance—a corroboree—and that I was part of this celebration. Maybe I was picking up what had really happened there, as I've always been very sensitive to the energies of the landscape, to the spirit of the land,' she reflects.

Over the years, Janet has learnt to hone her awareness when she's out in nature, so she can absorb as much as she can. 'Even when I'm returning to a place I know, I try to be blank as if I've never been there before, so I can be more receptive. In zen terms, it's called beginner's mind. That's when each moment is blank and ready to be felt. There's one particular rock I visit that I've had different reactions to. Sometimes when I go there the rock is sleeping, so it's not active. Sometimes at night-time you can't see it, you can only feel it. It's lovely to "paddle" on its back. It feels like childhood joy. You just want to lie down on it and cuddle it. It's a joyful, playful rock.'

Not all rocks Janet has come across have filled her with joy. 'I've been to other locations with Aboriginal elder Uncle Max, where there's granite boulders that have great meaning and strength,' she tells. 'There's one rock I had an adverse reaction to. I saw it at a distance and started to feel apprehensive and fearful. As I approached, I felt constricted in my heart. I actually started crying. Uncle just put his hand on my shoulder, not saying anything. He understood. I left that place as quickly as I could, as it was so emotionally powerful, but not in a negative way.' Like people, different rocks and their fairy caretakers have different personalities and energies. Looking back, Janet felt this rock helped amplify something in her she needed to feel, even though it was a bit challenging at the time.

The more we tune into nature with a pure heart,
the more willingly it will respond.

The more we tune into nature with a pure heart, the more willingly it will respond, deepening our experience of life and helping heal those parts of us that are out of balance. Some time back, I had an unexpected trip to the giant rock at Uluru after a bout of latent pneumonia. From the moment I was out in the desert, I could feel my life energy returning. Then as I stared up at this vast sacred rock at the heart of Australia's red centre, I was surprised to have it speak to me. This mighty rock explained that to be truly powerful, I needed to live more profoundly within my self and be who I was meant to be 100 per cent of the time. This, it explained, was why it had survived so long, when so much around it had not. This vast sacred rock went on to explain that the more authentically each of us lives, the more reason we have to celebrate the absolute fullness of our lives, and the more we're able to inspire others. This, it claimed, was why people found being around it so powerful. At the time, life had begun to overwhelm me. I'd become scattered, trying to do too much. I was so grateful this beautiful sacred rock reminded me there were other ways to be.

None of these insights are new to people who live close to the land, because they already have an intimate relationship with nature and its fairy keepers. They have regular access to so much wisdom.

A few years ago, I would have scarcely given rocks and stones much thought, beyond admiring them for their texture and beauty. Yet if an everyday person like me, who has lived most of her life in the city, can have a profound relationship with rocks, stones, pebbles and their resident fairies, there's no reason why you can't too. When you listen—really listen—to rocks and stones, there's so much healing to be had for each of us and for our fragile planet.

Sacred Rocks

Every piece of this impossibly intricate fairy jigsaw puzzle offers new ways of seeing and being in the world. Sometimes the new perceptions that come our way do so in the most unexpected places. A few years back, I visited the National Museum of the American Indian in Washington, DC. At the time, rocks and their fairy caretakers couldn't have been further from my mind. When I arrived at the museum, I discovered that in the planning stages, four rocks were chosen to sit outside the building, each representing one of the four sacred directions—east, south, west and north. Together with a fifth stone, which stands in the centre of the museum, these rocks were chosen to help 'anchor' the building in the land, and to bless and protect it.

These giant stones were chosen by native peoples in the far east, south, west and north of the Americas. Mirroring our own cycle of birth, youth, adulthood and old age, the rocks represented the different periods of earth's life cycle. Every part of the process was treated as sacred and undertaken with great care. Each stone was carefully dug up without being reshaped, polished or cleaned in any way. This meant that any living plant or microscopic creature on the stones was left where it was. There was no destruction of the land from where the stones were taken. When each stone was removed, it was replaced by a piece of the Kasota limestone used to build the museum, thus ensuring the stone's original landscape would remain in balance.

Acasta stone, the oldest known stone on earth, was used as the museum's northern marker. Found north of Yellowknife in Canada, this sacred stone represents the planet in its youth. Before it left for its new home, a Tlicho elder named Henri Simpson performed a special ceremony, to honour all this stone would bring to the planet in its new Washington home.

The southernmost marker, signifying the earth during its adolescence, was found in Tierra del Fuego, southern Chile. The Yagán people there, the southernmost native community in the world, selected a large boulder. For countless generations, this boulder sat on a slope looking northward across the bay to Argentina. Before it was taken to Washington, the community farewelled this giant stone and community president Patricio Chiguay said, 'This stone is a symbol of our people. Our people are slowly vanishing, but this stone will be our ambassador to Washington.'

The eastern quartzite marker stone was taken from Sugarloaf Mountain in Maryland and is believed to contain healing powers. The stone faces the Capitol Building, to encourage healing energies there.

The western marker stone, an 'a'a lava ball from the Hawai'i Volcanoes National Park, was the youngest of the four stones selected. The Hawaiian kipuka people believe that pohaku stones are living beings, so the chosen stone will be returned to Hawaii after twenty years, to be replaced with another rock or 'relative'.

Once the stones arrived at the museum, great care was taken to respect and protect them. Then on the first full day of summer in 2004, a solstice ceremonial blessing took place. Each native community offered prayers honouring these sacred stones. I would not have visited this museum had a friend not told me about it, but I was so moved by the energy there I burst into tears the moment I stepped inside the building. This museum is a truly sacred space, reminding us that when we make the effort to open up to living nature and her fairy caretakers, many blessings are likely to follow. Like all sacred moments, my day at the museum and all I learnt there remains close, lighting my way forward. In the busyness of everyday life, it's easy to forget that rocks and stones help anchor the land, enabling its creatures, plants and trees to thrive.

When you pay attention to rocks and stones, as the National Museum of the American Indian did, you can achieve some wonderful outcomes. When you fail to do so, things go awry. There are many dramatic stories of stones being taken from sacred sites without permission with all kinds of misfortune following. This is not so much about superstition as understanding that when the delicate balance of a place is disturbed, life loses its flow.

So before you move stones of any kind, ask permission of their resident fairy, as they know best where that stone is meant to be. If the fairy spirit agrees to the stone being moved and is happy with its new position, so much the better. Once you have the stone in its new location, welcome the stone and its fairy caretaker, and ask if anything else is needed, so the stone can continue to bless the land it occupies.

The question isn't so much whether
you believe in fairies,
as whether fairies have reason to
trust you with their secrets.
Fairies do not waste time on those
who have no love for them.
They can help you if they so choose,
but only if you have
sufficient wisdom and love to
respect what they offer.

Waking Up the Spirit of Clay

My quest to discover as much as I could about fairies has been full of surprises. When I caught up with ceramicist Janet Selby over a cup of tea, I was enchanted by all she revealed about clay. 'Most people go to a shop to get clay, then bring it home and unwrap the plastic,' she told me. 'I tell my ceramic students that it's essential to connect with the clay, as it's part of Mother Earth, and to honour the fact that it's come on a long journey to be with them.

'When someone unwraps the plastic wrap, they are often the first human to touch that clay. Millions of years may have gone into making it. The clay may have begun as a granite mountain, and perhaps over time weathering has washed the particles down into a valley. As clay is formed through the forces of nature, each place where clay is found has a different character. When a seam of clay is discovered, a machine comes along and digs it up and takes it away. It is dried, crushed and filtered. It goes through a processing machine that churns it around and adds some moisture. Next it is put through a mechanical pug mill. When it comes out it's then wrapped in plastic, and we buy the clay from a shop.

'Clay is amazing. Before you can use it, you need to wake the clay up. Clay has this remarkable plasticity. Before you throw it on the wheel you need to pick up the unopened bag of clay and drop it on the floor, making it more jelly-like. Clay definitely has a living spirit. Potters who work with clay on the wheel know this, and will tell you clay has a memory. If you're throwing clay on the wheel and what you're trying to create doesn't work out, you try again and again. But then the clay becomes tired and won't work for you. You might as well put that clay aside and recycle it into another batch, otherwise you just have more problems.

'If you make something on the wheel and you push the clay down because you're not happy with it, somehow the clay remembers what you have done and it might not then go the way you want it to go. I tell my students to make friends with the clay and avoid tiring or overworking it. It's about knowing when to stop and when to get a new piece of clay.

'Before you use the clay on a wheel, you need to prepare it. You need to cut it into the size you want and knead it. Potters have been doing this for thousands of years. Technically, this aligns all the particles of the clay, then it's easier for the shape to form. For me, this kneading process is more spiritual, because I put my imprint, my essence into that clay. I'm introducing myself to the clay, so we know a little bit more about each other before I begin to work with it. So for me, working with the clay is a spiritual practice.'

As I left Janet's studio, I felt so inspired by all the experiences she so willingly shared. I was astonished to discover that clay has its own memory, that it can become weary, and how much easier potting is when the potter has a relationship with the spirit of the clay. Yet again, there were some powerful clues about reaching out and connecting with living nature.

BIRTHING SOMETHING NEW
FAIRIES ARE PRESENT IN NEW POSSIBILITIES
AND ALL CREATIVE MOMENTS.
THEY LOVE THE JOY AND EXCITEMENT
THESE EXQUISITE MOMENTS BRING.
SO WHETHER IT'S A BABY, A NEW PROJECT
OR SOMEONE GETTING MARRIED,
DON'T FORGET TO INVITE THE FAIRIES IN.

When Mountains Call

Not long after I realised fairies take care of rocks and stones, I discovered that mountains also have their own resident fairy. These fairy beings are often referred to as 'devas', because of their vast size and the depth of their wisdom. Devas aren't your run-of-the-mill fairy. They're mighty beings, who oversee whole species or major life forms. When you connect with a deva, you're in touch with a highly evolved being. Mountain devas may oversee the welfare of a single mountain or a whole mountain range. They work constantly to help everything that lives in these mountainous places to flourish. Devas deserve great respect. They're incredibly powerful, and have lived long and know a great deal.

If you wish to connect with a mountain deva, it's important to slow down a little. Become silent and still. Then as you soften and relax, you're more able to access the higher states of aware-ness we touched on earlier. As you let go your expectations of how things might unfold, who knows what beautiful moments may be yours?

When you connect with the fairies
layer upon layer of beauty and deep wisdom is yours.

Entrepreneur Julian Noel told me of an exquisite experience he had with a mountain deva, which moved him deeply. 'I was on a retreat over Easter,' he explained. 'It was the last day, so we spent the time contemplating and meditating. Then as we were leaving, I looked across to this mountain in the distance and distinctly heard it call out to me, "Come and be with me. Come and be with me." So I said to my partner Jacqueline, "I've had this sudden feeling we should go to that mountain." She was happy to go along with this, so we jumped in the car and headed in the general direction of the mountain. It must have been a good hour away. We made our way towards the mountain without quite knowing where we were going. As we were climbing the road up the mountain, the air became stiller and stiller. It got to a point when we were about three-quarters of the way up the mountain when there was this incredible stillness. I turned to Jacqueline and said, "Wow, can you feel that?" She looked at me and nodded. There was this tangible sense of calm.

'When we got to the top of the mountain, it turned out to be a tourist spot. There was a car park and everything. But I kept following my intuition. I was told, *Walk over here. Turn here. Go up this path* and so on until we got to this place where I was told to sit on a certain rock, which we did. Then this voice said, *Meditate.* I told Jacqueline what I'd heard, and so we meditated. We went very still and calm. Then I had this image where I saw all this straw and hay piled up over my heart. It made me feel very sad, because I could see what was covering my heart. Then I heard the mountain say, *Give your sadness to me*. This beautiful "Yes!" welled up inside me. But then out of nowhere this wind came up, and I felt like it went right into my heart cavity and lifted all this hay and straw, and flung it off into the air. It just scattered it, and my heart was now this very pure energy. I just sat there.'

You don't have to come back to a mountain physically,
just come back to this place in your essence, so
it can give you its strength and its magic.

JULIAN

'Then the mountain began to talk to me some more, thanking me for coming. As I sat there, there was this gentle wordless conversation. The mountain said to me, *You know I've so much to give, so many gifts*. So we then began to explore these gifts together—the mountain's solidity, his groundedness. He explained that mountains were important because they were of heaven and earth. Then the mountain said, *People used to come here all the time, and I would give them of my gifts, but people don't come here anymore*. He asked me, *Will you please come back?* It was really funny because I suddenly panicked and thought, "Oh no! The mountain's asking for a commitment, and I don't know when I'll next have time to come all the way down here. Where's my diary?" The mountain kind of nodded and laughed, saying: *You don't have to come back physically, just come back to this place in your essence, so I can give you strength and I can give you the magic I have*. So I said, "Yes, I'd love to do that." And part of the way I now reconnect to the mountain is to retell the story.

'My understanding is that the earth has so much to give us and there are certain places that are magical, which resonate with the purity of our own heart. Our job is to stay connected to that pure place within, because when we're connected, then we're just guided to these magical places to sit and receive, and allow things to blossom. After a little while our conversation was over, so we walked back to the car park. Right by the car was one of those little tourist plaques, which told the history of the place. It said that up until white settlement, before the place was turned into a ski resort, all the local tribes would gather and spend summer on the mountain. I suddenly realised what the mountain meant when it said *people used to come here*. These local people would spend time on the mountain in the summer and really be there, so they could receive the mountain's gifts. But now they don't come anymore, not in that deep sense, and so they miss out. Speaking to the spirit of the mountain was an incredibly special experience. It was so amazing and humbling. It makes you realise how much we don't get, because we don't connect.'

This moving account of Julian's time with the mountain spirit takes us way beyond our narrow way of seeing the world. It leaves us in awe of what's possible, when we're prepared to take a leap of faith and stop and listen. We're so used to doing everything on our own, we have little or no real sense of the beauty and wisdom that enfolds us. Yet it doesn't have to be this way. I learnt recently, for example, that in many ancient cultures the mountain closest to where you are born is your sacred mountain. Isn't that a beautiful possibility?

What special insight might this hold for you? Perhaps it's time for you to connect with the spirit of your birth mountain, and see what it has to reveal.

What the Land Remembers

It's not just the spirits of trees, rocks and mountains that have something to share. So too does the spirit of a place. This isn't news to those who live close to nature. They already enjoy a deep relationship with the spirit of the land, which has been nurtured over generations. They readily greet the land and converse with it as you would someone you love. Today we're so busy and distracted, we rarely think about such things. Yet the spirit of the land still tries to reach out to us.

When you hear what the land has to say, you see and experience more than you could ever dream of. This happened some time back while I was visiting Scotland. It was so special for me to be back on Scottish soil, as my father is Scottish. I hadn't been to Scotland for years and regrettably, my knowledge of Scotland and my Scottish heritage was vague at best. But the three days spent visiting friends in the Highlands changed everything. In that pristine location, the land spoke to me in the most extraordinary way.

The spirit of the land holds our story and potential.

From the moment I arrived in the Highlands I felt a powerful sense of belonging, although I'd never been in that part of Scotland before. The place was strangely familiar, as if a buried memory had finally surfaced. I felt the spirit of the land reach out and embrace me. It was like meeting an old friend. I was so moved by this. It left me with a profound sense of belonging. As I walked the land, I felt a great and terrible sadness in my bones, as if some forgotten part of me remembered Scotland's painful and bloody past. The curious thing about this experience is that I hadn't read up about the bloody history of the place. I wasn't even thinking much about Scotland's past at the time either. I was simply enjoying the rugged beauty of the landscape. Yet remarkably, the terrible hurt and destruction of former times came flooding into my awareness in short grabs. It was like watching snatches of a movie in my inner eye. I was amazed at how vivid some of these experiences were.

Alongside these desperate images of loss and betrayal, an unexpected sweetness emerged out of the awful pain I'd witnessed in my inner eye. All at once, I could see how this wild unrelenting landscape had shaped its people, how it had encouraged the Scots to be strong, regardless. My soul danced to realise that it was out of this unforgiving land that my warrior self had been forged, and I now carried its powerful legacy with me in my cells. Even more remarkable was the realisation that no matter where on the planet I was, I could still access this strength whenever I needed it.

In those three days, I came to see how the land and its past, and my own story, were inextricably bound together. I knew that neither time nor distance could break this bond. Through this experience, I finally understood why the land is so important to the people who have occupied it for countless generations. I now know without a shadow of a doubt that the spirit of the land holds our story and potential through time. Our mission is to connect deeply with our story, and to make something worthwhile of it. Having experienced the land so profoundly, I was desperately sad to leave it behind so soon, until I reminded myself that I carry this place with me always.

It's been fascinating to discover how powerfully the land speaks to others who were able to connect in and truly listen. Bridgette, a young American archaeologist and writer, told how she'd been very moved by her time in the Highlands. 'When I'm in nature, I really respond to the landscape—to the spirit of the land,' she tells. 'I really, really react to the Highlands and the oak woods there, to the point where I get teary. I respond to the history of the land. I can just feel it. In Scotland, it's supercharged for me. It's like I can feel the weight and depth of the history. I love it. It's a strong sense of comfort. For me, it's an expansive experience. It's like I belong in the Highlands. I feel hugged by the land there. I'm in awe of it at the same time, because it's very old. But why should I love Scotland? I don't know. I just have to go and live there. I want to see what this landscape will do for my work and writing.'

Having been on a number of archaeological digs, Bridgette has had the chance to immerse herself in a number of very different landscapes, and has had some intriguing experiences with the spirit of all of these locations. 'I was in charge of this excavation near Niagara Falls,' she explains. 'It was great. We found pottery and all sorts of things. Then I moved away to Australia after two phases of the excavation. Even before the third and final part of the dig started, the third dig didn't feel right. The land wasn't welcoming. It didn't want us there. You could just feel beings watching you. As it turned out, the land didn't get disturbed with the third part of the excavation because of funding and things. A close friend had also felt what the land had been saying. We were both pleased this patch of woods was left alone. It was not meant to be touched and it let us know that.'

Some days it felt like the woods and trees were welcoming.
The branches parted easily for you.
On other days, it was like they'd hit you in the face
and made it as difficult as possible for you to be there.

BRIDGETTE

As Bridgette and her team got to work in those woods during phase one and two of the dig, they began to notice all kinds of nuances around the different places they were working. Sometimes the vibes changed from one day to the next. 'Some days it felt like the woods and trees were welcoming. The branches parted easily. On other days it was like they'd hit you in the face, making it difficult for you to be there,' she tells. 'My friend who was with me noticed the same thing. The spirit of the place was just not happy with you. It wasn't the time to be doing something there. When you're an archaeologist, you deal with nature all the time. Sometimes the weather's really hot, sometimes cold. You're used to that. But this was different. At times, this part of the woods didn't want you there. You almost felt like someone was tugging at your sleeve as you worked, like you had no space. Other days it was easy as.'

As Bridgette has become more attuned to the spirit of the land, she's found she's able to draw great strength and healing from it. She finds herself in an ever-deepening relationship with the land, as it offers her its wisdom and nurture.

These connections with the land can be extremely powerful. Frequently, some neglected part of us is healed when the land and its fairy caretakers communicate with us, as entrepreneur Julian Noel discovered. During his childhood, Julian spent most of his life away from his own Maori culture and homeland in New Zealand. Yet Julian experienced a deep sense of belonging when he finally returned. 'When I went back to the land where former generations of my whanau had come from, I hadn't been there for 25 years,' Julian tells. 'But as I rounded a bend, it was like a silk handkerchief had dropped over me. There was the most incredible stillness. I just knew I was being welcomed home by the land. It's like the land has a conversation with you. I went to the land of my grandfather's line and really loved it there. It was so beautiful.

'But after a few days I felt the pull to move on, so I went up to Hokianga Harbour, which has got to be the most exquisitely lovely place in the world. You're travelling through this mountainous hilly terrain, then you come to the top of the hill with no concept of the beauty that's about to explode in front of you. There's a massive great sparkling blue harbour with no buildings, just these gorgeous big golden hills of sand, ringed by incredible mountains. It was such an amazing explosion of beauty that it caused this tremor in my heart. Even though I felt more connected in this place, I was a little bit uncomfortable with my reaction. I worried I was being disrespectful of my own tribal lands. I kept thinking, how can I love this place more? How can I feel more at home here?'

The land remembered me, and I remembered it.

JULIAN

'After a few days, I was drawn to move on again. I went to this place called Matauri Bay. I had the same amazing feeling again, while standing in this little babbling brook. I'd come from the beach with bright blue skies and water, to the inland where it's thick with trees and fertile and moist. There was that beautiful musty smell of the earth with magnificent totara trees all around. I was there by myself and I just had to take all my clothes off and jump in the water, and this language came out of me. It felt like Maori, even though I don't speak fluent Maori, and I thought, "This is how the land wants to talk to me." So I just stood there feeling really great.' After these experiences, Julian went back overseas.

'Years later, I met one of the elders of my tribe,' he explains. 'I told him how I was drawn to the Hokianga and to Matauri Bay, and how I'd had a strong reaction to them but didn't understand why. He told me my grandmother, who I never met, came from the Hokianga, so half my family line was from that area. He also told me that Matauri Bay is where my tribe, the Ngati Porou people, lived before we came to the Kaihu Valley. I was blown away. The land remembered me, and I remembered it.'

Since that experience, Julian has given his connection to the land much thought. 'Quite often when I drive through Northland where my ancestors are from, I swear I see the spirits moving across the landscape and I just feel really comfortable with that,' he tells, adding, 'I know it's not fantasy. There are spirits in the land. They're really beautiful, benevolent energies. I felt there was a calling there, a benediction, a deepening, an initiation from this whole experience.'

Julian's experiences say it all. No matter who we are or what we may or may not have achieved, you and I are part of something inextricably intricate and profound.

OBSESSED BY A FAIRY TALE, WE SPEND OUR
LIVES SEARCHING FOR A MAGIC DOOR
AND A LOST KINGDOM OF PEACE.[13]

Eugene O'Neill

Fairy Helpers

It's very humbling to realise just how often fairies try to make contact. How much energy they expend in attempting to console, delight and uplift us. As you develop a relationship with the fairies, you become more aware of their presence and assistance. You start to see or sense when they are close by. 'Often the way fairies communicate with me isn't actually through words—it's a feeling,' explains Renee, a young graphic designer who's been dealing with the loss of her mother to cancer. 'Sometimes the fairies will put a memory of something that's happened in the past in my head that's relevant to me now. I've found that if I'm upset about something, they'll pull something funny out of my memory to lighten the mood and show the absurdity of the whole situation. Fairies want our energy to be lighter and happier. That's why they try and make you feel better.'

Sometimes just to see a fairy is enough to bring comfort. Lisa was feeling distressed after a family argument when she saw her first fairy. To her surprise, this rather regal-looking fairy emanated an overwhelming sense of kindness. 'You could see her feelings reflected in her eyes—love and compassion for the pain I was going through,' recalls Lisa. 'She didn't seem to be that aware that I was staring at her in shock. She seemed very absorbed with me, focusing on my pain. Eventually she realised I was staring at her, then disappeared, but I continued to feel her presence.'

This unexpected meeting had a real impact on Lisa: 'Since my encounter, I've been outside in nature more than ever and try to do my part to help the environment.' Like many who have encountered fairies, Lisa has also made a habit of picking up other people's garbage, because she can't bear to see the beautiful earth despoiled. Lisa has also made her own fairy garden, to celebrate the presence of fairies in her life. 'Now I know without a shadow of a doubt that fairies do exist,' she says, adding, 'it has changed my life forever. It has even has made me feel closer to God.'[14] This is another insight often shared by those who encounter fairies. They develop a much deeper, almost mystical connection with the divine.

It wasn't until she was 79 years old that Marian saw her first fairy, who appeared at just the right moment. 'I saw this wonderful red rose in my friend Robyn's garden,' she explains. 'There was just one rose on the bush and Robyn kindly cut it for me, even though I didn't want her to. However, I was very pleased to have this dark red velvety rose. It was intoxicatingly perfumed. When I got home, I put it in a vase and placed it on the coffee table in front of me. It lasted and lasted and, as the days went past, it got bigger and bigger. I kept expecting the petals to drop off but they didn't. And then in the middle I saw its golden centre.

'When I looked closer, there was a tiny being sitting up with her arms held out to me. I blinked and rubbed my eyes, but she was still there. This lasted several days. The fairy was leaning a bit further forward each day. I really thought I was imagining it. At the time I had a small surgery ahead of me, which I was worried about. But as I looked at this tiny figure, I realised that a real sense of peace had come over me. I just didn't think about what was lying ahead. I was filled with a peaceful elation instead. Then the first petal fell. Gradually the petals fell off one by one, and my little fairy friend was gone. I've no doubt this was a special message for me. I have had friends who have seen these little people, but this was my first time. Wasn't I so lucky?'

When I looked closer, there was a tiny being
sitting up with her arms held out to me.
As I looked at this tiny figure, I realised that
a real sense of peace had come over me.

MARIAN

You don't have to live in the country to make contact with fairies. Artist Roshilla lives in the crush of the city and still sees her fairy friends. 'The fairies come to me in my apartment, if I'm feeling lonely,' she tells over coffee. 'They're a real comfort. They let me know they're there. They'll pull my ears or play with my hair. Here I am living in the middle of a city of millions, and sometimes I can see all their faces. This is one connection I'll never let go. I can feel them and on a good day I can see them.' She went on to tell me how challenging adult life had been for her, and how much comfort she's gained from having fairies in her life.

Though Nicolette was born in England, she has lived most of her adult life in Australia. While she loves her new home, she really misses the change of seasons and the deciduous trees of her childhood. 'I grieve for woods and cool weather and green,' she admits. 'So I try to create as much green as I can in my garden. I've filled it with flowers, and my basil and all the green things I can. Wherever I can, I place a stalk or anything that will grow in the soil.' Little by little, Nicolette has created a green haven in her lovely pocket handkerchief garden, to help keep her close to nature and the fairies. Nicolette's inner city garden has been a great balm to her in the inevitable ups and downs of adult life. 'I don't see fairies as pretty little beings with wings,' she says. 'I see them more as butterflies, which is interesting, as I always have a lot of big butterflies in the garden.'

Bridgette, an archaeologist and writer, also gets a lot of help from fairies. 'The fairies really come through for me when I write,' she explains. 'They're very much in my inner eye. I have a fun room where I write that looks out onto nature. When I write, I don't so much dream up the characters as they present them- selves to me. I'll be sitting there, and I can almost see a fairy sitting on a plant pot swinging their legs. The fairies are very visual for me then. When I write, I feel the individuality of the beings around me. That's when I get the more tangible aspects of fairies. But when I'm in nature, it's more like I feel them around me. When I'm in nature, I feel a healing, comforting presence from them. I've also felt their curiosity about me and what's going on, a sense of being watched in a very relaxed kind of way. At other times, I've felt a playfulness and a lightening of mood.'

Now Bridgette has become used to this fairy presence in her life, she's not afraid to ask the fairies for help. 'I know to go into nature when I need to and ask for healing,' she tells. 'Often when I've shut my eyes, I've seen fairies around me with my inner eye, cleaning my energy.' Now Bridgette has begun to appreciate fairies and all they do, she's sometimes able to help them out as well. 'One morning I was walking in my favourite park, and someone had had a party there the night before. There was rubbish everywhere,' she recalls. 'I felt inspired to clean it up. As I was tidying up, I felt their presence thanking me and buzzing all over me. They were so hurt that someone would abuse their space, so they asked me to help out. Even though it was a lot of work, it became playful. Their happy energy was all around me.'

Seeing a fairy is a life-changing moment—a moment whose meaning sometimes evolves over time. Linda had been struggling with a candle-gazing technique in a meditation class, and was a little disappointed to see everyone around her having amazing experiences. 'A few weeks later, I decided to take a candle into the bathroom and take a bath in the pitch black, to give this candle gazing another go,' she tells. 'As I lay back and stared at the candle, I found myself much more relaxed. The darkness certainly created an impressive backdrop. About twenty minutes passed. As I lay there, I noticed a small flicker of gold light appear on my left. It moved across towards the candle and seemed to rest on the top of the flame, which looked like a thin laser beam. The beam became approximately three inches tall, then started to expand, then it closed again.'

A body of gold light filled the centre of the wings …
This fairy stayed and continued to
allow me to observe its beauty.
I watched quietly until it left as it had
come, with a flash of gold.

LINDA

'I watched quietly, keeping as still as possible, unaware of what the light was. As the golden beam of light opened again it split down the centre, giving the impression of gold wings of light, then closed again. Then it changed colour. It started from the bottom with violet and blue, then the colours went to green, then yellow and orange, finally blending into a vibrant pink. All the colours were electric. As the light opened again, I could feel an emotion from the being. It felt hesitant, cautious, almost coy. It seemed as though this being was watching me and talking with me telepathically. The wings opened and closed slowly several times. A body of gold light filled the centre of the wings and I asked, "Are you a butterfly?" Instantly, I felt the answer was no, they were a fairy. This fairy stayed and continued to allow me to observe its beauty. I watched quietly until it left as it had come, with a flash of gold. The whole experience took at least ten minutes. I have not seen a fairy since then and have not tried to. This was an event that happens when it's supposed to. I will remember it always and still feel the true reason is yet to be discovered.'

Thanking Fairies

As you immerse yourself in the world of fairies, it's easy to get caught up in what fairies can do for you, forgetting to honour them for all they bring to our lives. Just like the rest of us, fairies need to know they're appreciated. One of the best ways to acknowledge our fairy friends is to live with a grateful heart. So never let an opportunity pass to thank them for everything they bring to the world. It's also important to realise fairies don't just appear or help us simply because we want them to. When fairies come into our lives, it's generally for a larger purpose. They hope that by helping us, we'll then take more interest in nurturing another part of creation, creating a wonderful chain of good.

There are so many beautiful ways to express your appreciation of them. In times past, people thanked fairies for their work with simple gifts of bread or wine. These gifts were chosen because they came from nature and could be returned to her with ease. There was also another wonderful aspect to such gestures. Once the wheat or grapes were harvested, someone had to work with love to make them into bread or wine. So in giving fairies bread or wine, people were giving something of themselves to the fairies as well. This is an important detail, because a rich life is about giving as well as taking, about getting your life energy moving and making an effort.

When fairies come into our lives, it's
generally for a larger purpose.
They hope that by helping us, we'll take more
interest in nurturing another part of creation.

Fairies don't have to have gifts of bread or wine to know they've been appreciated. A loving heart fills them more than you might imagine. Fairies also delight in beautiful things, because beauty feeds them, as does any creative act. You may like to acknowledge the fairies in your life by painting and drawing or playing music. Or when next you're in the woods or by the seashore, why not create a small circle of stones? Or weave together a handful of twigs? Perhaps assemble a small pile of pebbles, shells or feathers, to quietly thank the fairy folk there. Do whatever captures your imagination. And don't forget that these and other lovely gestures nurture the spirit of a place, allowing even more good to flow into the world.

Fairies at Work and Play

Eager to discover as much about our fairy friends as possible, I've dipped into ancient tales of fairy encounters. Many told of glimpsing fairies dancing on mounds and hillsides, in meadows and woodlands, which left me wondering why fairies loved certain locations so much. My sense is that fairies are drawn to wherever life is most vibrant and to pristine places where energy is naturally heightened.

Fairies dance as they work, because they're in the flow. They love what they do. That's why it's impossible for fairies to separate work from play. They live in the heart of creation, where life is pure energy. They dance just as the atoms dance. Fairies relish the endless movement of energy through the living world and are energised by it.

Fairies also love order, because without order everything would descend into chaos. The whole of creation relies on their attention to detail, their ability to maintain balance and beauty in nature. As fairies nurture life in all its forms, they also oversee the process of death and decay, willingly assisting the never-ending cycle of life and death.

Fairies dance as they work, because they love what they do.
It's impossible for them to separate work from play.

As they lovingly tend the particles of life, fairies weave them into intricate patterns, helping birth plants and trees, grasses and lichens, and a myriad of life forms. So much depends on their unselfish devotion to creation. Miraculously, it's no burden for fairies to do what they do, because they love nature unconditionally. Fairies take great joy in the many particles they work with, as these are the building blocks of life itself.

Sensitive to the world around them, fairies are constantly adjusting to whatever is happening in the environment, so they can help nature thrive. When conditions are favourable, the patterns fairies work with help keep the world in balance and also create new life. However, when the fundamental patterns of life are disturbed or harmed in some way, all the fairy effort has to go into healing these distortions. Many of the imbalances they have to deal with have been created through human thoughtlessness and pollution. Put simply, our carelessness makes a lot more work for them.

As nature's builders and caretakers, fairies work with the sacred blueprints of life itself. Each 'specie' of fairy has its own unique blueprint to work with. A dandelion fairy works with the dandelion blueprint. The devas are like giant architects, and oversee and protect the blueprint for each specie. Each deva protects and nurtures a single specie, helping that specie to thrive. Devas are highly evolved fairy forms; some suggest they are part of the angelic hierarchy. Findhorn's Dorothy Maclean and many others have communicated with devas on numerous occasions.[15] Devas are also the guardians of the accumulated wisdom and evolutionary path of a specie. They also monitor global conditions and take careful note of how these factors impact on the specie in their care, then respond accordingly.

We owe a great debt of gratitude to devas, as they bring much good to the world. It is the devas who oversee the work of countless nature spirits. Through precise instructions from their deva, fairies carry out their own specific tasks in nature. Once a fairy has been given the responsibility for a certain rock, plant or tree, they take up residence there, devoting their whole life to that rock, plant or tree.

The work of the nature spirits is intricate. A great deal depends on their accuracy. Yet the busy little nature spirits do not mind their painstaking tasks. They give their all to what they do. Nothing is too small or insignificant for their loving touch. Some of the energy patterns these fairies work with are so fine, they're almost like mist; while other patterns look like spectacular bursts or swirls or showers of light.

Light is also an important element that fairies work with, as light is essential to life. Everything that lives is imbued with light. That's why life-giving radiance constantly flows through fairies into all of creation. Light helps bring everything to its fullness. So whenever you spend time around plants and trees and feel energised, you're benefiting from this same life-giving light, which fairies have in abundance.

Living Outside of Time

In the glimmering world of the fairy, there are no divisions between the past, present or future. In these timeless realms, there are freedoms we can scarce dream of. This place beyond time is often spoken of in fairy tales, and in the numerous accounts of those who have met fairies, who often tell of having lost all sense of time while with them.

Mama's no-nonsense mother-in-law shared her own fascinating story about her unexpected encounter with the 'little people' and about entering a timeless space. The old lady grew up in the Pacific Islands as a very young girl, and spent her days playing in the fields, while the men worked the sugar cane. One day she wandered off and came across the 'cutest little people'. Tugging at her dress, her tiny friends began to laugh and play with her. Enchanted by these new playmates, the child didn't hesitate to join in their play. As it turned out, the little girl was 'missing' for two days and nights. Unaware of the passage of time, she was busy playing with her intriguing fairy friends without a worry in the world. Years later, when the old lady saw her grandchildren playing in the same spot, she was concerned they too might 'disappear'.

In their timeless realm,
the fairies experience freedoms we can scarcely dream of.

Sometimes time slips aren't so much about seeing fairies as experiencing their timeless world. A couple of years ago, I had a curious experience on the outskirts of the city. It was late afternoon and a blisteringly hot, dusty day. I was sitting in my car at traffic lights, when suddenly the road and all the surrounding cars vanished. I found myself on a slight rise in among sand dunes and spiky spinifex grass. As I savoured the caress of a warm summer wind on my face, I was struck by the pristine beauty of the place. I knew instinctively I was being allowed to glimpse how this place had once been, before the natural landscape had been bulldozed and covered in bitumen and buildings. The beauty and silence there were so profound, they were balm to the soul.

Then just as quickly, I was transported from this time long gone. I was back in my car with whole lanes of traffic on either side of me. After all the tranquillity and loveliness, it was a shock to realise just how much of the land's natural features had been obliterated. Yet remarkably, the memory of this place remained through time, held no doubt by the spirit of that landscape. Now and then I find myself back at those same traffic lights and, whenever I'm there, I reconnect with the ancient memory of the place and am exhilarated and saddened to remember how the place once was.

In these and other precious moments when we slip through the cracks of time, we enter the enchanted slipstream of life where everything is effortless. We touch the divine. There in that sacred space, we see beyond our doubts and confusion to a space where anything is possible. Freed from the narrow confines of time, we find ourselves in a much more expansive landscape, where we can see or experience the spirit of a rock or tree, a plant or place. We enter a space where dreams can come true.

When we enter the enchanted slipstream of life where everything seems effortless, suddenly we feel as if anything is possible.

Science confirms that time is fluid. So if you want to improve your life, a good place to start is by changing your relationship with time to enable it to be more free-flowing, just as it is for the fairies. How can you do this? At present, too many of us are imprisoned by deadlines and endless commitments. This will shift once you understand that time is a moveable feast, because you're living at a more cosmic level, where everything just is for all of eternity.

Now and then, we all travel backwards and forwards through time in our thoughts and dreams. And have you noticed how responsive time is to how you're feeling? When you're stretched and stressed, time seems to press down on you, making it almost impossible to do everything that's needed. And when you're angry or unhappy, time stretches endlessly and painfully before you. However, time dissolves when you do what you love. Suddenly, a moment of unexpected joy seems like never-ending bliss. All this and more is possible, when you tap into the fairy realms.

Molly, a medical professional who lectures all over the world, works closely with the fairies to help her manage her time. 'The fairies have taught me a lot about time,' she explains. 'Some days you panic, wondering how you're going to fit everything in. But then when you understand quantum theory, the power of thought and things, you start to see there's more to time than you realised. I ask the fairies for their help when I have a lot to produce in a very short space of time, and it really helps. I've also noticed that if you're doing something you really love, they'll stretch time for you, so you get the full benefit of it. But you have to ask them.'

As you get a sense of how else to experience time, new door-ways open up. It's the perfect opportunity for you to consciously choose how you wish time to be. If you respond to time posit-ively, it offers you endless possibilities to make your heart sing.

IF YOU SEE THE MAGIC IN A FAIRY TALE,
YOU CAN FACE THE FUTURE.[16]

Danielle Steel

Fairy Magic

One of the many things that puzzle us about fairies is the knotty question of what fairies really look like. Some people see fairies who look exactly like the fairies in children's fairy tales. Others glimpse very abstract, ethereal fairy figures. Yet others have glimpsed some very strange-looking fairies, whose features and dress mirror the surrounding landscape. Does this mean some people are seeing fairies, and others are seeing quite different beings?

As you sift through fairy accounts, you begin to realise that when a fairy decides to make themselves known to you, they often choose a body and clothing which reflects the images you already have of fairies. For fairies, this process is a bit like picking an outfit from a wardrobe. As there are lots of illustrations of fairies in books and films, there are plenty of possibilities for fairies to work with to help you recognise them.

But this isn't how fairies really are. At their essence, fairies are 'light beings'. They happily take on a fairy form you're comfortable with, so you can spot them more easily. Then when the fairy encounter is over, the borrowed fairy body and clothing dissolves, and the fairies revert to their essential selves.

While fairies may dress up for us so we can recognise them,
those who encounter fairies often sense
how very different their life energy is from our own.

It's fascinating to see how this plays out in everyday encounters. Lucille, a busy grandmother and healer, had a wonderful fairy experience when she was out in nature, which could have been straight out of a storybook. 'I saw a big lizard with little people riding it,' she tells. 'They were little elves about a foot high. They were just smiling as they were riding along. I was gathering flowers to make flower essences at the time. There were lots of fairies around me, as I worked away. They were hovering around and being part of things, helping me. They were little flittery fairies, just like the Bib and Bub drawings I'd seen as a child. When I tuned in they kept saying to me, 'We are one, we are one.' Isn't it intriguing that in the midst of this lovely fairy scene, Lucille's fairies were directing her beyond how they looked to who they were at their essence?

What's also interesting is that even when fairies 'dress up' to look how you expect them to be, people still sense that their energy is very different from human energy. Rashuan had been visiting relatives and was walking back to the car, when a small white object flew past. Surprised, Rashaun stopped short and extended her hand without thinking. A tiny fairy in a 'white feathery dress' and no more than an inch and a half tall landed on her hand, then lay there looking up at her. The fairy didn't have distinctive features but looked like a person. When Rashuan lifted up her hand, the fairy flew away. Rashaun describes this little being as 'not like a person, but with person-like qualities'.

Lisa had a similar experience when she saw her first fairy. At the time she was very taken with the fairy's 'regal' demeanour and brown skin. This gentle being had beautiful, dark chocolate-brown eyes. Yet even though this fairy stranger was pleasant to look at, she caught Lisa off guard, as she didn't look like any of the fairy illustrations Lisa had grown up with. Lisa's lasting impression of this fairy was that while she was very lovely, she wasn't totally human.[17]

Fairy stories are a rich source of information about the fairy realms, when we learn to read between the lines.

One of the fairy encounters that stood out for Clive was when he caught sight of a green male figure around four feet high sitting in a tree. After looking at this fairy figure for a while, Clive suddenly realised he was only seeing what he thought a fairy looked like, rather than how this fairy really was. So the next time he was out in the woods and sensed there was a fairy around, he asked the fairy if he could see it as it really was. He then saw a large white cloud over a group of trees. 'As I tuned into this cloud it coalesced and flowed down becoming more concentrated, and eventually presented itself in front of me in the form of the fairy-tale fairy,' says Clive. 'She was very beautiful and was quite amused with our encounter. I felt privileged to be in her presence, to see her as she really was, and then to see her as she chooses to be recognised.'[18]

Another reason why fairies like to change their appearance is because they love new experiences. Fairies are very curious as well, so they quite like experimenting. Many fairy tales tell of fairies summoning sumptuous feasts, fine horses, musicians and fantastic castles out of thin air, vanishing as quickly as they appear. All this and more is possible, as fairies know the laws of matter intimately. What is clear is that fairies can draw things out of the ether with ease, then as effortlessly cause them to vanish. The more you discover about the quantum universe, the more you see how this fluidity gels with what we're learning about fairies. I now believe fairies work with matter at the quantum level. When you contemplate this possibility, you begin to get a sense of the workings of life on a whole new level.

Fairies have been granted access to the building blocks of life, because they can be trusted to use it unselfishly. Working closely with their deva, they're very careful about what they bring about, because they know just how fragile the web of life is. Apart from moments of pure fantasy and enjoyment, fairies devote themselves to living nature and to helping it to thrive. Sometimes they bring things into being simply for the pure joy of experiencing them, and because they love any and every opportunity for playfulness and imagination. Unlike humans, they don't feel the need to hang onto the things they manifest, because they know this would only impact on their lightness of being, weighing them down.

I suspect one of the many insights fairies offer is to never hold on too tightly to what life brings our way. This isn't always so easy to achieve in our material world. Yet if you and I could create just a little more lightness of being, life would be less burdensome. People and situations would come our way with greater ease, as would new ideas. Imagine if you spent your days exploring new ways of being alive, like the fairies do? That you recognised everything you experience as a gift from life itself and were deeply grateful for it?

All these possibilities and more await you, when you choose to follow in the enchanting footsteps of fairies. Then you will become the magic you ache for.

Make-Believe

When you think of fairies and the magic they have at their fingertips, it makes you curious about the mesmerising world of make-believe. But what is make-believe, and what can you learn from it?

For fairies, make-believe is an everyday occurrence. It's what they do all the time. They believe in their ability to create things and they do. Each and every day, fairies dream up wonderful possibilities. Sometimes they manifest things from a sliver of an idea, sometimes with a grand plan. And because they believe dreams can come true, they help make it so. How different life would be if you and I could do the same!

So how does make-believe work? To ensure their wishes come true, fairies think in detail about what they seek to create. They only begin to shape a wish when they believe in it with every fibre of their being. Then they infuse their wish with as much beauty and goodness as possible, to ensure what they're about to create won't harm life in any way.

The formation of a wish is intricate work, which is why fairies lavish their wish with as much love and attention possible, until it feels complete. This process of bringing a new idea into being takes time and close attention to detail, but fairies never shy away from the detail, because they know it's an important part of the process. And as every wish has a life of its own, the fairies also willingly infuse their wish with a little of their own precious life energy, to help breathe life into their wish.

Fairies work on their wish until they know the shape and feel of it intimately. Yet they're also careful not to want their wish too much, lest the weight of their expectations smother their fledgling idea. As their wish begins to take shape, fairies remain focused on their wish in a positive relaxed way, surrounding it with as much love and light as they are able. Then when they feel the time's right, they draw their wish gently and lovingly out of the ether and another dream comes true. Part of a fairy's ability to make things happen is because they believe wholeheartedly that wishes can come true. They are deeply grateful whenever this happens, and see their wish for the tiny miracle it is.

All wishes emerge from the ether, from the gossamer-thin substance that enfolds our physical world. It's here in the ether where all thoughts and ideas reside. Once shaped, a wish lives on in the ether, waiting for the moment when it can come to fruition in our world of form. If you could see how many thoughts are floating around in the ether, you'd be amazed. Here these ideas stay, until someone draws them out of the ether and into our everyday world.

Ideas happen in all kinds of ways. Sometimes you may dream something wonderful up. At other times, ideas may find you. It's easier to attract wishes and inspiration your way, when what you love aligns with a wish already in the ether. Put simply, from time to time you attract some wishes a bit like a magnet, because you share the same energy. With a little love and care, you may then help draw the wish out of the ether and into our world of matter.

Many of the thoughts swirling around in the ether are formed by where our attention is on the planet. The thoughts may be informed by what we watch for entertainment, what we read, what we talk and obsess about. So like the fairies, it's important to be aware of where our attention goes, because every time we focus on specific thoughts and ideas, we give them a little of our life energy and help bring them to life. Then when the next person encounters those same thoughts in the ether, the thoughts grow a little more through that person's attention. Should an unhelpful thought or idea slip out, be sure to change it into a positive one. That way, you'll never add to the darkness in the world.

Wishes are like babies, they need a lot of time and attention. And if you want your fledgling wish to take flight, only share it with those who care. It's all too easy for your wishes to be crushed by the envy, unkindness or ignorance of others. It's also essential you believe in your idea, and not waver in your belief. If you can't hold the dream, it's not going to happen.

Nurture your new wish and, if the conditions are right, you may help birth yet another exquisite possibility. Even the tiniest wish can bring great light to the world. So why not use your ability for make-believe to create a world of lasting beauty, inspiration and joy?

Dark Times

Fairies are aware of the pain humans sometimes feel,
but they never allow it to leave its mark
on them, and they ask we do likewise.
Sometimes dark things do happen,
but try not to dwell on them
as they will only feed off your
life energy, draining you.
Instead spend your time with people and
in places that make your soul sing.
And let the fairies help heal you with their
inspiration, kindness and generosity of spirit.

What No-one Tells You About Wishes

When you look a little closer at fairy stories, you discover some intriguing clues as to how wishes are best formed. Have you noticed that when fairies offer to fulfil someone's wishes, they often grant the person three wishes? Have you ever wondered why three wishes? This question puzzled me for some time. Then when I delved a little more deeply, I discovered the significance of the number three. Threes are evident in our life cycle—in birth, life and death—and in the way we divide time into past, present and future. There are also three special fairy trees—the ash, the oak and the hawthorn.

Three is also the number for creativity and birth. Three represents divine perfection and the divine child full of promise. It's no accident that there were three shepherds and three wise men at the birth of baby Jesus. Threes also hint at the ancient link between fairies, angels and humans. To arrive at the number three, you add one (masculine) and two (feminine) together. This creates three, the divine child full of promise.

It's also said that whatever you put out into the world will return to you threefold. Should you be granted three wishes, you're being gifted something very special, so think carefully about what you wish for. If there's something you really want, it helps to request it three times, to activate its full potential.

When granting a wish, a fairy taps a person's third eye,
so they can see clearly into a situation.

Some stories tell of fairies granting a wish by tapping a person's brow with their wand. Why would they do that, you may ask? A fairy taps a person's brow to activate their third eye, known also as the loving or discerning eye. Your third eye is very important in wish-making, as it helps you see further than your everyday eyes can. It may even help you glimpse the distant past or the future. So by tapping your third eye, a fairy is offering you the chance to choose wisely by seeing clearly.

Fairies are often depicted holding a wand, topped with a five-pointed star. The number five represents humankind. It also signifies earth, air, fire and water, the precious elements from which all life is formed. The fifth element is spirit. When you make a wish with the point of the star reaching heavenwards, you're inviting all the elements of life to be present in the form-ation of your wish. Hopefully, you are also infusing this new wish with an added blessing, by asking that it reach its best and highest manifestation. Of course, fairies don't need wands to make wishes come true. Nor do you. Wish-making is all about intent and focus, about imagining your heart's desire clearly and in detail. It's also important to direct your life energy towards your wish and to nurture it, to enable your wish to take shape.

Wish-making is serious business, as every wish you draw out of the ether alters the world in some way. Before you make a wish, think carefully about how it may impact on you and others. Be clear about whether you want this wish fulfilled. Is it because it will genuinely enhance your world in some way, or because you've grown needy or become lost in the expectations of others? A good barometer is to ask yourself whether your wish will help you and those around you to feel more loved, more inspired, more at peace.

Many stories tell of fairies granting a person's wish, on the condition they're given something in return. This may seem a strange request, given fairies can magic up things out of nothing with ease. But there's another important law of life at work here. Fairies know well that receiving must be balanced with giving. So when a fairy helps make a wish come true, it's very important you honour this gift by giving something in return, and by keeping your end of the bargain. This way the balance of life is maintained. Should you break your promise or fail to give back, sooner or later things will go awry, because the natural order of things has been disturbed.

Wish-making is serious business, as every wish you draw out of the ether alters the world in some way.

There are times when fairies bestow something on a person or household, asking for nothing in return. Sometimes fairies do this because a person may not be in a position to give anything back. Or perhaps that person is in need of a lucky break. Or a fairy may simply be trying to demonstrate that goodness has its own rewards.

Whatever the bargain you strike with the fairies, make sure you keep your word, even if you have to give up something you love. Never shrink from doing what you know in your heart is right, even if a small sacrifice or inconvenience is required. Keep your word and you will be rewarded many times over.

Don't Wish the Rain Away

As you start to look at the world in new ways, you begin to see how much of our everyday world is built on our wishes and dreams. Like the fairies, you also have more than a touch of magic at your fingertips. So never doubt your power to make things happen. The flip side of this is to be clear about your thoughts. It's so easy to get sidetracked by all the wishes you'd like fulfilled, and forget about the many unconscious wishes you make. Your unconscious wishes can also come true, impacting on you and those who come after you in ways you hadn't imagined. So tread with care.

Few of us have any idea of the effect of hundreds of thousands of city dwellers waking up to the rain, and wishing it away. Living divorced from nature as most of us do, it's easy to forget that the rain waters the earth and fills the rivers, enabling our plants and trees to grow. Year in year out, the rain washes our streets and cleans the atmosphere, bringing with it the sweet gifts of green meadows, plenteous harvests, lush forests, singing brooks and spectacular waterfalls.

Few of us have any idea of the effect of hundreds of thousands of city dwellers waking up to the rain and wishing it away.

So the next time you wake up to the rain, instead of wishing it away, why not open the door and step outside to greet it? Perhaps it's time to tiptoe through puddles, bathe in the falling rain or walk barefoot on the wet earth. Allow yourself to experience the soft drip of rain on your skin. It's important to embrace the rain when we can, because you never know when it will return. I'll never forget the astonishing chorus of birds I heard when rain finally came after years of drought. It was incredible!

Fairies know the immense importance of such things. They see how alive plants and trees and the earth feel when the rain comes. They rejoice in the way the soft patter of rain, the gentle embrace of mist and the insistent drumming of a tropical downpour thrill the natural world. These and a hundred other invitations are extended daily for you to become exquisitely and completely alive. Don't be too quick to dismiss moments that might at first feel a little uncomfortable—allow their gifts to reveal themselves to you.

The Glamour

There are so many aspects to the make-believe worth exploring. Frequently in fairy tales, you come across talk of 'the glamour'. But what does it mean? The glamour is a veil of illusion cast over a situation, person or place. Basically, the glamour allows someone or something to appear differently to how they really are.

Those versed in enchantment use the glamour to appear stronger, to seem more alluring and more powerful than they are. Yet as spellbinding as it is, the glamour has little to do with reality. It takes a lot of life energy to create and maintain an illusion. That's why glamour usually only lasts a short while. To maintain glamour is hard, because illusions need to be fed with a lot of energy. So it's good to be wary around anything glamorous, as it can drain your body and spirit.

Those versed in enchantment use the
glamour to appear stronger,
to seem more alluring and more powerful than they are.

One of the many attributes of celebrities is their glamour—the elaborate illusions they use to get noticed. While it may seem an attractive way of life, it's pretty taxing, because glamorous people will soon find their life energy alone is not enough to maintain the illusion they've built up around them. Desperate to keep up appearances, they start to draw on the life energy of others to feed their glamour. Like vampires, glamorous people suck the life energy out of anyone and everyone they can. As their glamour grows, so too does their need for more life energy. Those drawn to a glamorous person give of their life energy every time they pay that person attention. The greater the 'diet' of other people's life energy, the more 'glamorous' that person will appear.

Glamour has a mesmerising quality to it as well. So as the glamour grows, more people fall under the glamorous person's spell and give even more of their life energy by worshipping their idol. That's why glamorous people need continuous attention. They rely on a constant stream of life energy from other people, to bolster them up. When hundreds of thousands of people freely give their life energy to a glamorous person, their presence becomes larger than life and extremely seductive, and may be hard to resist. In time this person may become a star, because they appear to shine more brightly than anyone else. Yet no matter how tantalising a star appears, their glamour can never last. And when their glittering illusion begins to fade, fewer and fewer people pay them attention. Their glamour fades and eventually they disappear from view.

There is another more profound way to shine. You can do this by nurturing your own inner radiance. Like the fairies, when you shine from the innermost part of your being, you illuminate everything and everyone around you. Often you will touch the lives of others without realising it, and without any effort at all. To shine, the only thing you need do is to live a life of goodness and unselfishness, and to surround yourself with uplifting people and situations which make your soul sing.

You know when you're around someone who is naturally radiant, because they light up your day, dissolving any sense of loneliness, sadness or near despair. This is in sharp contrast to those with a glamorous facade. You may experience momentary euphoria on encountering someone glamorous, but the buzz will soon fade, leaving you empty inside and out. Once you understand the dynamics of the glamour, it's much easier to see through it.

When you're in balance, radiance flows through you in a constant life-giving stream. Love is the key, if you want to attain true radiance. Love for yourself, for others, for all living things. When you imbue everything you do with love then, like the fairies, you will begin to shine with a radiance that need never fade.

When Everything Is Not As It Seems

As alluring as the fairy world may be, everything is not as it seems, so you need to take care always. When you step into the fairy realms, you can't rely on your five senses alone, as it is a place that has its fair share of illusion too. Fairy tales remind us constantly not to take what we see at face value, but to look into the heart of things. So before you seek out life's enchanted places, it's important to listen to your intuition and use your inner sight, so you can discern those things which are good and true amid those which are not.

You'll know when a fairy trickster comes calling,
because your life will be turned upside down.

When you view life through your inner eye, you save yourself a lot of anguish, because there are many tricksters in the fairy realm. In these dazzling realms, sometimes those who seem most attractive prove to be cruel, foolish or untrustworthy; while those who are true may come to you in disguise, appearing desperately poor, or hard to love. Some of these other-worldly tricksters are relatively harmless. Others can cause you serious pain.

You'll know when a fairy trickster comes calling, because your life will be turned upside down. A fairy trickster may help you laugh at yourself, change direction, or may prove extremely destructive. While no-one likes to have a trickster appear on their doorstep, these mischief-makers can help wake you up and avoid even more painful lessons. Good, bad or indifferent fairy tricksters challenge you to take stock, to question what you value. They help you appreciate what you have, and recognise what you no longer need.

A fairy trickster may be kind or cruel, someone who is fiercely intelligent or seemingly stupid. Other-worldly tricksters are often hard to gauge and can throw you off balance, because they can display opposite qualities at the same time. So they may be generous and selfish, or surprisingly loving one moment and icy cold the next. Should you encounter a trickster, it's best to centre yourself, then listen to your intuition to help you sum up the truth of the situation.

Tricksters come into your life to force you out of old routines. They're challenging, but they can be great (if uncomfortable) friends. They help nudge you out of old and unhelpful patterns. They demand courage and the will to change. They may take you way out of your comfort zone. This may sound seriously scary, but it's not as daunting as staying stuck. Sometimes you have to disappoint others to be true to yourself, to speak out when it would be easier to remain silent, or to brush off the dust of the past and set out on a new journey alone.

Frequently, your initial reaction to a trickster will be fright, anger or despair, because this isn't what you'd hoped for. This is a natural reaction. But don't be dismayed or hold back from this opportunity, because in letting go of what you no longer need, you'll liberate yourself from all the stuff you're carrying that makes life challenging. Your new path may be painful or uncomfortable at first. Don't panic. These are just 'birthing' pains and they will pass.

Equally, a trickster may appear if you've become complacent and take people or situations you hold dear for granted. It's only when the trickster arrives, threatening to take those things you love away from you, that you wake up. The situation may resolve itself easily, or you may have to fight tooth and nail to reclaim what's yours. When a trickster comes calling, it may not be a comfortable time, but it may just prove the perfect moment to make the changes you ache for, or to wake up and hold fast to what truly matters to you.

Not all fairy scenarios are so exacting, but they may still require you to look beyond the obvious. Fairy tales are full of stories of beings who are not what they seem. In these spellbinding tales, you meet the wise old woman who at first glance appears foolish, or the prince who walks the world as a beggar. By using your inner eye and listening to your heart, you begin to see a person's true self. Then maybe, just maybe, one or two miracles will flow from these insights.

Following the wisdom of your heart doesn't always mean you get to see the full picture—at least not at first. But it will point you in the right direction. Walter Yeeling Evans-Wentz was an American anthropologist who collected numerous tales of fairy encounters. He tells of a Pat Feeney, who had an old lady come to his door in need of some oatmeal. Pat offered the stranger potatoes, but the old woman insisted she have some precious oatmeal. She asked Pat to leave her some oatmeal in a bin, so that she could collect it later, which he did. The next morning when Pat inspected the bin, he couldn't believe his eyes. It was 'overflowing with oatmeal'. It was only then that Pat realised the woman must have been a fairy in disguise.

Being open to messages from the fairy realms holds us in good stead. However, accessing this wisdom does involve daring to venture out of your comfort zone now and then. Roshilla, a city-based artist, finds that whenever she's out of balance, a fairy messenger helps get her back on track. 'Last year I kept seeing this extraordinary girl looking at me in the street,' she tells. 'I couldn't stop looking at her, even though everyone else ignored her. Then one day she spoke to me saying, "You're connected to Mother Earth. You belong to her." She was very beautifully dressed. In the moment she spoke to me she was very real, then she vanished into thin air. This happened right here in the city. I've had a few instances like that.'

So when next you meet someone you don't know, look a little deeper and you may be surprised by your encounter. Always try to treat strangers with kindness and respect. Use chance meetings as opportunities to practise your generosity of spirit and to stretch your capacity for goodness. To master this art is a great gift, because when you do so, you will access a heightened awareness the fairies are so familiar with and begin to walk in fields of gold.

WHEN THE FIRST BABY LAUGHED FOR THE FIRST TIME,

ITS LAUGH BROKE INTO A THOUSAND PIECES,

AND THEY ALL WENT SKIPPING ABOUT, AND

THAT WAS THE BEGINNING OF FAIRIES.

AND NOW WHEN EVERY NEW BABY IS BORN

ITS FIRST LAUGH BECOMES A FAIRY.

SO THERE OUGHT TO BE ONE FAIRY FOR EVERY BOY OR GIRL.[19]

James M Barrie

Our Not-So-Everyday World

As I slowly began to piece together some of what I'd learnt about fairies, I began to get a more intimate sense of their world and to see that theirs is a place of great beauty, beyond conflict and sorrow, with other-worldly colours and music that are almost impossible to describe. As I pondered these exquisite attributes, it began to dawn on me that one of the many gifts fairies bring is to help us see our world through their eyes. They help us begin to appreciate the true loveliness our everyday world holds, to see that we are living in a sea of miracles.

Fairies are mesmerised by our everyday world, because they see the never-ending dance of atoms. They marvel at the rivers of light beneath the land that flow out in all directions, bringing life and vitality to all who dwell there. And when they look at you and I, they see the many exquisite ways in which particles of matter have been lovingly woven into flesh and blood. Fairies are also enchanted by the intricacy of the human body, home to our spirit. As they go about their days, they joy in our light, our limitless potential. Fairies see our ambitions and dreams as clearly as if they were their own. They also see how the shadows of the past often weigh heavily on us.

The secret is to live like fairies,
as harmlessly, lovingly and intelligently as we can,
so we too can help create heaven on earth.

As our physical world is denser and slower than that of the fairy realms, fairies are also amazed by our ability to thrive on a planet which often seems a little leaden to their's by comparison. Our world is less vibrant than theirs, because it lacks our love and attention. In part, that's why our colours are less vivid, our music less harmonious and the scents in nature are muted. However this need not be so. With careful attention to the earth, you and I can experience the world the way the fairies do, full of beauty and endless potential.

Some people have already glimpsed these possibilities in moments of heightened awareness, or by simply taking the time to sit and observe nature. One of the most powerful examples of what is possible took place at Findhorn in Scotland, where plants and trees flourished beyond expectation, and where flowers bloomed in the snow. At Damanhur, the amazing eco community in Italy, you can also glimpse what's possible. Residents have discovered ways to 'teach' plants to harmonise, improvise and create music. They're now working on a way to create tree houses, which can be in tune with their environs and with the subtle energies found there.[20]

As we ponder these and other delicious opportunities, how can you and I help bring tiny miracles about? How can we experience life in all its loveliness and potential?

Wishing Trees

There's so much you and I and everyone can do, to join the dots and realise our dreams. In times past, trees and their fairy caretakers have helped make wishes come true, and they still long to do so. This opportunity is still open to those of us with wishing trees.

First, you need to find your wishing tree. If you aren't already aware of a wishing tree, take a look around your neighbourhood for a tree that has an enchanted feel. You'll know a wishing tree when you see it, as it will fill you with a sense of expectation and pure delight. You may find there's a wishing tree tucked away somewhere in your garden, your local park or in nearby woods.

You can tell when there's something special going on with a tree, because whenever you're around trees you truly resonate with, you feel more relaxed, more inspired. You feel like almost anything is possible and, in recognising this, you help make it so. Should you suspect you've happened on a wishing tree, there are many wonderful possibilities awaiting you. But a word of caution here. Be careful not to rush in and spoil things. First, you must get to know the tree and its resident fairy. Take the time to reach out with a pure and grateful heart, so that you can work together to create something beautiful, something of worth, not just for yourselves, but others too.

It's important to give your special tree and its fairy caretaker your loving attention, even if it's only a few moments here and there. Note the tree's roots, its trunk, its branches and leaves. Note all the tiny creatures that use the tree for food, for their home. Loving attention is the key here. It's only after you've developed a loving relationship that you can even consider asking the tree to help you with a wish.

If you don't have a wishing tree nearby, you may like to plant one in your garden. When you've selected your special tree, be sure to find somewhere that's slightly hidden from view, as life's miracles often flourish best in quiet unexpected places. Once you've planted the tree, don't forget to continue to love and nourish it. And take care never to burden the tree with your expectations. A tree must always be loved and cherished for its own sake.

In times past, people would whisper their wish to a wishing tree, as they placed their hands on the tree's branch or trunk. By making gentle contact with the tree, they developed their own beautiful relationship with that tree through love and kindness. This practice of touching trees is where our expression of 'touch wood' comes from—that moment when we touch something made of wood, in the hope that something we wish for will happen.

There may be a tree in your garden or nearby
park or woods which has an enchanted feel,
and may prove to be a wishing tree.

When you touch a tree respectfully, you help create a bond with that tree and its resident fairy. When making an actual wish, some people like to walk three times around a tree, then three times backwards, keeping their wish clearly in mind. You may feel more comfortable simply asking the tree for help. Once you've made your wish, be sure to listen carefully to what the tree fairy has to say. It may tell of the special circumstances needed to make your wish come true, or advise how to fine-tune your wish in some way.

The instant you whisper your wish or speak it out loud is a precious moment. So when you do so, you might like to mark this by hanging a coloured ribbon on a tree branch. Then whenever the wind blows, it can take up your wish, and carry it far and wide. Whatever your wish, use it wisely. The best wishes are those which benefit others, as well as yourself. Should your wish come true, don't forget to thank the tree and its fairy caretaker, who have worked hard to help make this little miracle happen.

Fairy Treasure

Fairies have countless treasures in their keeping and can magic up the riches at will, and see into the heart of things. Unlike humans, it's much easier for them to hold what they possess lightly. It is true that fairies love silver, gold, and precious stones, but not for their status or for what they can buy. They love these precious metals and gems for their life-enhancing properties. They treasure gold, because it radiates the vibrancy of the sun. Fairies love silver, because it radiates the sweet feminine energy of the moon. Fairy folk prize precious stones for their healing properties and their power for good. If you are wise, so will you.

Fairies know the true value of diamonds for their ability to help you gain clarity and express all you hold in your heart, while emeralds are much prized as bringers of peace. Emeralds can also help you find your unique voice and express your creativity. These remarkable little stones can also mend the gaps and tears in your energy field, and gently assist you to find your way forward, when you feel a little lost. Rubies offer protection to those who hold them close. They help you find strength and courage, and assist you in serving others, even when you feel you've nothing left to give. Fairies hold dear these precious stones and many other treasures.

Fairies love silver,
because it radiates the sweet feminine energy of the moon.

For too long, humankind has been envious of fairy treasure, without understanding its true value. Life in the numinous realms was never about power and status, but about beauty, wisdom and healing; about how best to reflect the divine in all things. So be wary of craving fairy treasure, or of being tempted to steal it, as such deeds never end happily. More than likely, you'll be left with a pile of ashes or a fistful of straw.

Some fairy stories tell of dragons and other fantastic creatures, closely guarding massive hoards of silver, gold and rare stones. Long ago, we are told, these fantastic creatures had vast amounts of treasure, which they guarded with their lives. While the thought of all that wealth was very enticing, few realised why these magnificent creatures gathered up sapphires, emeralds and rubies, and towering piles of silver and gold.

Dragons were not motivated by avarice, so much as the opportunity to nourish themselves and their young. Sadly, their healing treasure troves made these magnificent beasts vulnerable. Their largesse was a temptation too strong for some of our ancestors to resist. They slaughtered these beautiful creatures for their treasure, and now these mighty beasts and all they know of life's enchanted ways are lost to us.

House Fairies

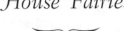

Fairies seek to help us access the spirit or essence of things. They want us to be whole, to live in a space of wonderment. Only then, can you and I be a real force for good in the world. As well as helping us enjoy a more intimate relationship with nature, the fairies would love us to become aware of the spirit of our home, as each house is a living place that has the potential to nurture us in all kinds of ways.

We transform our homes by paying more attention to the energy there. Note how the feel of your home space is affected by what happens in it, from the people who visit, to everything that's discussed and experienced there. All the love, the moments of sadness and joy, the daily frustrations and unexpected miracles are woven into the bricks and mortar, and remain there through time as a living record of all that has taken place within those four walls.

As you ponder these possibilities, it's thrilling to discover that no matter how grand or dilapidated your home, it has a resident house fairy who faithfully tends it. You can help your house fairy maintain the living fabric of your home by lifting the life energy up a notch or two. By enjoying loving meals. Making time for fun and laughter. Listening and caring for those who live there. Creating a nurturing space. By maintaining and cleaning your home with love and grace. All these positive energies and more make it much easier for your house fairy to take care of your home environment.

No matter how grand or dilapidated your home,
its house spirit continues to tend this
structure until it is no more.

Before my journey into all things fairy, I'd never considered the possibility of house fairies. But it didn't take long to warm to the idea, or to find others who'd experienced them. 'I have fairies in my house where I'm living,' explains city-based artist, Roshilla. 'I always have lots of candles and fast music around me, as fairies love fast music. I leave out honey and little lollies for them, which they really like. Sometimes I can hear them talking. They talk very quickly. They do all sorts of funny things. They move my things around. They make me laugh. They also look after the energy of the house.'

One of the loveliest ways to support and honour your house fairy is to make a small offering of thanks each day, or whenever you're able to. You might like to do so with a flower, a handful of nuts, a thimbleful of wine or beer, a prayer, or any other uplifting gesture that comes to mind. It's always good to give your house fairy something that's meaningful to you—a tiny sacrifice, like sharing a piece of good cheese or chocolate. House fairies deserve something special, because of the tireless work they put into the energy of your home. If you do give your house fairy some food, don't eat it afterwards, as fairies extract the living essence from the food, leaving no nutritional benefit. House fairies love these and other thoughtful gestures, because they increase the positive energy they have to work with in your home.

House fairies work hard to inspire you to add all kinds of loving touches to your home.

Sometimes it's hard for house fairies to do their work, because our homes are cluttered, neglected or sad, leaving the energy clogged and heavy. You've probably noticed how when you get busy and distracted, stuff piles up and your home feels less inviting. House fairies love everything to sparkle, because this raises the energy in your home. There's great wisdom in the expression: *Cleanliness is next to godliness*, because when you clean your home, you give it a big energetic lift. It's amazing how vibrant and inspired you feel after your home's had a good clean. Suddenly you feel as if anything's possible. The higher the energy, the more space for new ideas, for relaxation, for feeling completely at home. So never underestimate the power of a good spring-clean.

Creative touches are also important to the energy of your home, because they help infuse your personal space with life. That's why house fairies inspire you to add all kinds of loving touches to your home, creating more joy and nourishment there. So pay attention to details large and small. And don't forget to savour each and every uplifting moment, from the bliss of newly pressed sheets and lavender in the linen press, to the delight of clean windows and freshly washed floors. These and a thousand other tiny gestures make your home more inviting, cared for and lived in, and help transform it into a true sanctuary.

With the help of your house fairy, you begin to see your home's full potential, and can then make a truly delightful space for yourself and those you love. It's a good idea to ask your house fairy to help you see your home with new eyes. As you look at your home more closely, you'll begin to see where the energy is lacklustre, often in areas you never use or those that are cluttered. Become aware of the places where you love to sit, and those you avoid because they feel cold or unloved. What can you do to make problem areas more lovely, more inviting? As you start to notice unloved rooms or forgotten corners, you'll see those spaces in need of more light. It may only take clean curtains or blinds, a lighter shade of paint, a mirror or skylight to turn these areas around. When you are more tuned into your living space and tend it, you will feel a dramatic lift in the energy of your home.

Your hearth is the living heart of your home and needs your attention. Many of us have forgotten or never knew that the hearth was where people in times past rested, enjoying its warmth and comfort. That it was around the hearth that people told stories of the day, mulled over the past and dreamt of the future. Your hearth is a beautiful space to decorate at Christmas and Easter, and at other special times of the year.

Look for your house fairy in the lightest part of a room.
You see them where the sunshine falls,
or where the light is reflected in mirrors and off surfaces.

A hearth is also an in-between space, a magical doorway between worlds. That's why, while sitting at your hearth, you may see other-worldly faces in the flames of the fire, or glimpse those who are lost to you. While seated at the hearth you can sometimes hear the comforting whisper of the wind down the chimney, or lose all sense of time; new ideas and special memories will come to you there without effort.

While most people are rarely (if ever) aware of their house fairy, these diligent little beings are never far away. Without their hard work and loving attention, it would be much harder to thrive in your home. If you'd like to glimpse your house fairy, look for them in the lightest part of a room. You'll see them where the sunshine falls, or where the light is reflected in mirrors and off shiny surfaces. They're also in those spaces that most inspire you—on a much-loved sofa, in a quiet corner, by a stained-glass window, or in those parts of your home that look out onto the garden or nature.

House fairies pay constant close and loving attention to what you do, what you hope for, and what your spirit needs, working out the best ways to make your home the life-enhancing space it's meant to be. House fairies try every which way to inspire you to appreciate your home also. It's your house fairy who prompts you to savour the appearance of the moon at a certain window in the dead of night, or to pause for a moment to watch the sunlight inching its way across a room in the late afternoon. These homely fairies speak to you through the comforting creak of old floorboards, or the rattle of a window on a stormy night. It is they who encourage you to move furniture, paint walls, or open the doors to let fresh air in.

House fairies also tend the structure of a home, the same way other fairies tend plants and rocks and trees. The longer you remain in one place, the more your house fairy is able to create a genuinely beautiful space where you and those you love can flourish. Over the years, you and your house fairy can develop a close bond. That's why older homes that have been cared for often have an inviting feel. These houses have been lived in and appreciated by their occupants and by extension their house fairies, for a very long time.

Life took an interesting turn for Verena Stael von Holstein, when she and her husband moved to a run-down watermill that had belonged to her in-laws. Verena and her husband took on the mill, planning to renovate. Not long after moving in, Verena met the house fairy, aptly named Miller. He was pleased to have them in the mill, as they planned to bring it back to life. As the relationship developed between Miller and Verena, Miller revealed that once the fairies responsible for the mill's decay heard about Verena's renovation plans, they'd moved on.

Verena actually saw the fairies responsible for the decay of the mill before they left. She describes them as looking like spider webs to her inner eye.[21] Over time, Verena and her husband made the mill their own. And as it turned out, Miller was not the only fairy tending the mill. He had a whole group of fairies to help him.

Your house fairy nudges you to savour the appearance of the moon at a certain window in the dead of night, or to pause for a moment to watch the sunlight inching its way across a room in the late afternoon.

It's easy to assume these little fairy beings are simple beings, unaware that many hold a surprising amount of knowledge and are a genuine power for good. When Canadian teacher and healer, Tanis Helliwell, decided to rent a cottage in a remote part of Ireland for the summer, she was in for a big surprise. The night she arrived at the cottage, cold and exhausted after her long trip, she had an uncomfortable feeling she wasn't alone. All of a sudden she saw a tiny man, his wife and two children staring at her out of the gloom. This little leprechaun told her that he and his family had lived in the cottage for over a hundred years. He said they'd allow Tanis to live in the cottage over summer, as long as she accepted their conditions. After Tanis agreed somewhat reluctantly to his terms, a whole world of understanding and information opened up to her that summer. This tiny leprechaun took Tanis into the heart of the fairy realms, where she got to experience a whole range of fairy beings, and to see the world through their eyes.[22]

Like most fairies, house fairies know you almost better than you know yourself. But as many of us now move frequently, it's hard for these busy fairies to build a rapport with us. When you do get to know your house fairy, you can begin to work with them, benefiting from the many tiny nudges they give you to paint a wall, remodel a room or add to your home in some way. When you've completed these improvements and sit back to enjoy them, it's important to say thank you, as always.

The aim of a house fairy is to bring a house into perfect balance, so it's a living, loving space. When you work with your resident house fairy, it's much easier to achieve this. It helps when you can do your bit by maintaining the structure of your home and filling it with uplifting experiences, as the bricks and mortar, the furniture and everything else you have in your home are then imbued with these qualities. Fun, food, laughter and the pure enjoyment of being with those you care about feed the living energy of your home, making it easier for your house fairy to do their work, and for you to thrive. Then your home will become everything you wish for, and more besides.

FAIRIES SING AND DANCE AS THEY WORK,
BECAUSE IT FILLS THEM FULL OF LIFE.
WHEN FAIRIES DANCE, THEY DANCE WITH THE ATOMS.
AND WHEN YOU CAN SING AND DANCE
WITHOUT FEELING SELF-CONSCIOUS,
YOU TOO CAN CELEBRATE THE INFINITE
BEAUTY, MAGIC AND JOY OF LIFE.

The Fairies in Your Garden

Gardens are also an important part of any home. If you want your garden to be truly special, again it helps to work with the fairies. Some years back, I was thrilled to discover that fairies work best when part of a garden is left undisturbed. The idea is to set aside somewhere in your garden just for the fairies. Choosing a dedicated space for the fairies isn't difficult, even in a small garden. Simply find a corner that's asking to remain hidden. If you spend some quiet time in your garden, you'll know exactly where this fairy patch needs to be.

I wasn't at all certain I had any chance of working out where my garden fairies would like to hang out undisturbed, but when I looked carefully at my pocket handkerchief garden, I knew immediately where the fairies wanted to congregate. The space in question had a rather mysterious, yet deeply comforting, feel to it.

If you're still wondering about this, let me assure you that when you allow fairies their own space, your garden will be quietly transformed and an occasional miracle may happen there, as the fairies are able to reside in their own special patch without any interference. There's so much potential in gardens, regardless of their size. As you start to build a rapport with the plants and trees in your garden, you'll also develop a rapport with their fairy care-takers. This enables these fairies to reveal to you all your garden is capable of. Fairies do this by inspiring you to plant a certain bush here and certain flowers there.

Sometimes fairies will talk to you through a sudden moment of inspiration. Sometimes they don't leave anything to chance. I was at a talk some years back on life after death. The speaker was busy contacting loved ones who had passed over, when suddenly she looked a little taken aback, as she gazed in my direction. 'There's someone over here who has fairies around them,' she said, then added, 'They love what you've done in the garden. They'd like you to think about a water feature as well.' Startled, but quietly thrilled to have had this communication, I thanked the speaker, who then returned to the topic of the evening!

As you work with your garden fairies, try to make your garden a welcoming space for yourself and other creatures in need of a home and some nourishment. You might like to make a place where birds can nest, or where tiny creatures can shelter. If you do feed the birds, hedgehogs and other creatures, make sure you give them food that's good for them, and allow them to take some food from your garden.

You might like to decorate your garden with fairy lights, as fairies love these happy pinpricks of light.

There's no end to the magic you can create in your garden, when you take time to add a few special touches. As fairies love water, you might like to make space for a tranquil pond, small fountain or birdbath. Or you may wish to create a little nook where you can sit in tranquil moments. You may even like to decorate your garden with fairy lights, as fairies love these happy pinpricks of light. Fairies also delight in wind chimes, whose beautiful melodies are carried far and wide on the wind. These and a thousand other inspired touches bring huge amounts of joy to our fairy friends, and uplift your spirits also.

Often there's a lot of work to be done in gardens. With the busy lives we lead, this can at times be a little overwhelming. When you're feeling this way, it's a good time to call on the fairies to help you do what you need to do in the best way possible. When you're gardening, it's a good idea to simply do one thing at a time. As you work away, give the garden your full attention, so that whatever you undertake is done mindfully. When you're working in the garden it's also important you enjoy your work. This way, your enjoyment flows from you through to the plants and soil. And always make sure your touch is light, as gardens are full of delicate possibilities.

When you prepare the ground for planting, give the plants and trees whatever nurture you can, so they get a good start. Feed and water them with care. Sometimes you may be tempted to try to force plants to flower or fruit before they're ready, and end up stressing the plant and its resident fairy. Plants are acutely aware of your thoughtlessness—just as you sense this in others—so be sensitive to their needs. Know that herbs, flowers and vegetables grown with love will nourish you far more than those grown purely for profit or to impress. It also helps to know that food and herbs grown in your garden or local area tend to be more beneficial than those brought from great distances, because local plants share your environment, experiencing the same opportunities and challenges. So if they're thriving, chances are they'll help you thrive as well.

Never underestimate the nourishment you can receive from homegrown fruit and vegetables. This is especially true of plants grown in the same location from seed; the life energy in these plants is often more potent than in plants that have been moved around. When the time comes to trim or prune plants and trees, make sure you inform the plant or tree what you have in mind, so their fairy caretakers have time to prepare that plant or tree for change. That way, the work you plan won't come as too much of a shock. The same is true of mowing your lawn or moving plants or trees. It's hard to explain the terrible fright plants, trees and shrubs experience, when things happen unexpectedly.

When the time comes to trim or prune plants and trees,
make sure you inform the plant or tree,
so their fairy caretakers have time to
prepare for these changes.

It's also a good idea to ask permission from the nature spirits, before you go ahead with your work. When you ask for their cooperation, make sure you listen to what they have to say, as their advice can make all the difference. You may discover it's better to do your work the following day or week, or not at all. This approach may seem unnecessary, as you have your way of doing things, but there's far more going on in a garden than you or I realise. When you work more closely with the fairies, you will get more done because you're not wasting your energy. You may discover that while your plans seemed fine, they are less than ideal because something unexpected is about to happen, which would undo all the good you're trying to achieve.

There are many wonderful ways to listen to the fairies in your garden. Take time to observe the plants and trees in your garden at different times of the year. Note which plants are thriving and where. Which areas in your garden are most comforting, and which areas need more tender loving care? Note how each tree blossoms and when, and where the very first daffodils appear. What do each of these details tell you about the land in your care? When you take note of these nuances, you touch the living potential of your garden.

If we build homes and gardens without much thought to the land and its fairy caretakers, our homes and gardens only ever have a superficial beauty. But if you look at the earth more closely, you'll begin to see how the life force moves through the land. And if you're lucky, the living spirit of the land may reveal itself to you and allow you to glimpse its potential.

I'll never forget the first time I glimpsed the spirit of the land. I was staying with friends in the country. It was early morning in winter and there was a chill in the air. As everyone else was still asleep, I was tempted to stay in the warmth of my bed, but I felt drawn to look outside. As I pulled up the blinds, I saw the landscape was swathed in a gossamer-thin mist, which hovered above the ground. Staring out at this other-worldly scene, I could see the life energy moving snake-like through the land, nourishing and blessing it. It was an electrifying, deeply moving experience. I could see the planting my friends had done was in perfect alignment with the land. This didn't surprise me, as they'd gone to considerable lengths to listen to the land, which in turn inspired everyone who visited there.

Take time to see where the sunlight falls in
your garden at different times of the year.
Observe the shady areas there.
What do these details reveal about the
spirit of the land in your care?

Sometimes we compromise these beautiful possibilities because of our impatience. Even though you may be fired up about your plans for the land in your care, try never to ask too much of it because, like you, the land has its own needs, including the need for rest and replenishment. As you begin to work with the land more closely, do so with a keen eye and open mind, so it can reveal to you what is most needed. Then once you're clear about what is to be done, give yourself totally to the earth as you work.

As always, it's essential to balance taking with giving. So feed the earth in every way possible with water and nutrients, and with your love. Then at your journey's end, why not give your body back to the precious earth? As the soil embraces your physical remains, it can benefit from the nourishment of your flesh and bones, and from the memories and wisdom you carry in your cells. When you gift yourself back to the earth in this way, you help nourish the future dwellers of that place. So give to the good earth as freely and lovingly as the earth gives to you.

Healing Notes, Perfume and Colours

The further I ventured into the fairy realms, the more intriguing the journey became. I began to see how every plant specie has its own unique song. Sadly, most of us will never hear these sweet melodies, because we're too distracted. Yet occasionally a plant will reveal its song. To hear a plant's melody, you must give yourself totally to a plant. Take gentle care of it. Love it with all your heart. Observe its every aspect. Then, if you are blessed, you may be gifted with the plant's song.

Those who have discovered one or more plant melodies tend to live deeply immersed in nature. Realising they have been given something special, they hold these precious songs close. The miracle is that those who have these 'songs' in their keeping no longer need to pick plants, to access their healing properties. All they need do is sing the plant's song, to bring its healing qualities to life.

As well as its unique song,
each plant specie also has its own healing scent and colour,
nurtured by its fairy caretaker.

Everywhere you look in the plant kingdom, there are exquisite details concealed within things, which at first glance seem ordinary. As well as its own unique song, each species of plant has its own healing scent and colour, which again is nurtured by its fairy caretaker. You've no doubt experienced the healing qualities of plants, through essential oils extracted from plants or in an aromatherapy session. What I didn't know was that along with each oil's unique perfume is a corresponding sound and colour. So when you apply an essential oil such as lavender, rose or bergamot, you're benefiting from its healing scent, as well as from the accompanying healing sound and colour of that essential oil.

The healing sound and colour of an essential oil depends on which part of a plant the oil is taken from. Oils extracted from the root or base of a plant tend to last only an hour or two. These oils have the deepest notes and are associated with the colours red or orange, which relate to the healing of sexual, survival and creativity issues. Oils taken from a plant's stem can last several hours, and have a higher range of notes. These oils correspond with the colours yellow or green, which help you move beyond issues around fear, being too much in your head, or having difficulties with personal power and being able to listen to your heart. Essential oils from the top of a plant, or from its fruit, can last up to a couple of days. These oils have the highest notes and are at the blue or violet end of the colour spectrum. They can help you with issues around speaking out, as well as connecting to your intuition and the divine.

Where a plant grows, its shape, form and colour can also indicate which parts of your body may benefit from its healing properties. So a kidney-shaped leaf may be beneficial to your kidneys, while a plant which grows in rugged terrain may help you regain your stamina or endure difficult times. Some rare plants grown in the searing heat of desert areas may help heal burns and remove radiation from your body.

This knowledge is not gained in a day, and is best left to those who have made a lifetime's study of plants, and who have learnt to work delicately and respectfully with a plant and its fairy caretaker. However, you can still delight in these exquisite possibilities.

The Leaves of the Shepherdess

As you explore the fairy domain, you begin to realise that when you return to a more profound relationship with nature and the nature spirits, remarkable things can happen. Nowhere is this more apparent than in the plant kingdom. Some years back, international teacher, botanical illustrator and ethnobiologist, Kat Harrison, had a break in the mountains of northern Oaxaca in Mexico. While Kat was looking forward to getting away to this remote area, she was worried about her heart. She'd always had a heart murmur, but was now finding it hard to breathe, so was keen to do ceremony with a Mazatec healer and the sacred plant La Pastora, also known as the Leaves of the Shepherdess. This sacred ceremony is not something undertaken lightly; it also needs the assistance of a healer who has an intimate and respectful relationship with the plant.

Each plant spirit is a being in their own right, who is to be revered, petitioned and thanked for their healing gifts.

KAT HARRISON

Each healer has their own special patch where they grow their healing plants. It is there, hidden from view, that the healers lovingly tend their plants with great care. They know when and where their healing plants may be used. The level of healing gained from these plants depends on the relationship the spirit of the plant has with the healer who cares for them. 'Each plant spirit is a being in their own right, who is to be revered, petitioned and thanked for their healing gifts,' Kat explains.

Having found a healer who was satisfied that she had a genuine desire to make contact with the spirit of La Pastora for healing purposes, Kat was invited to join a sacred ceremony with the healer and his family. Before the ceremony began, the old healer warned Kat that the spirit of La Pastora was extremely shy, so Kat had to be very quiet and still. She was warned that if someone moved or spoke suddenly, La Pastora would vanish. Kat was also told she needed to be very clear about what she hoped to gain from this ceremony, and be open to what the ceremony might bring. She was also instructed to pray, 'to really pray and listen'.

As the ceremony got underway, Kat greeted the spirit of La Pastora. Introducing herself, she asked that her heart be healed. She also requested she be given a sense of the way forward in her work and life. Then as Kat settled back to wait and see what happened, she became aware of the countless generations before her, who had petitioned this beautiful plant spirit and benefited from her wisdom. All at once there was a shimmering and Kat found herself in 'another world', in a lovely garden near the forest, where there was a female being twenty feet high. Kat was amazed to find herself standing in this garden, staring up at an exquisite woman who had butterflies and hummingbirds flying around and through her.

The sunlight streamed through La Pastora as she tended her garden. As Kat gazed at this beautiful figure, she so longed for La Pastora to touch her. It was only then that Kat realised she couldn't move, but she could sense the presence of the old healer and his family, who were also taking part in the sacred ceremony. To her surprise, she suddenly realised they were now plants in La Pastora's garden. When finally La Pastora reached out and touched her, Kat describes La Pastora's hands going through her 'like a breeze, like a ripple' and in that instant, Kat knew she was healed. Kat also remembers 'inhaling and exhaling' La Pastora's presence.

A little while later, there was a second exquisite experience. 'When she passed her hand through my chest a second time, I saw a tiny ornate wooden door in my heart,' Kat recalls. 'It was carved with flowers and vines, and had an intricate golden fili-greed handle and hinges. As her grand spirit fingers brushed it, I felt a strong breeze open the tiny door and a pocket of hurt blew away.'[23]

It's in truly sacred experiences that you begin to glimpse the immense beauty of the fairy realms, and the many remarkable beings there. These and other profound moments are gifts, which live in our hearts forever.

Wounded Earth

Sadly, not all aspects of nature are lovely right now. Significant parts of the planet are struggling. Our thoughtlessness is putting our fairy friends under huge pressure. This terrible wounding of the earth mirrors our neglect of ourselves and each other. Instead of being grateful for our lives and the beautiful world we inhabit, this period of unprecedented prosperity has left us even more depressed, self-centred and needy.

This way of life is unsustainable. We need to discover newer, more profound ways to live and repair the damage we've created. The earth and her fairy caretakers need our help, love and commitment to turn this heartbreaking situation around. So as we look to the future, it's vital we think about what we want for the earth, and how best to enter into a more intimate relationship with nature.

Sometimes we may despair at the work needing to be done to heal the earth, as the damage is so great. But it's important not to lose heart. Nothing is impossible, especially when we work with our fairy friends. They are quick to remind us that with loving care and attention, beauty can find a home in the most desolate of places. So as you begin to size up what the land in your care needs to heal, call on the resident fairies for their help. They already know in minute detail what needs to be done, to bring the earth back into balance.

The miracle is that when you heal the earth,
something inside you is also healed.

Before you start work on the land, spend some quiet time with the wounded earth. Take a moment to invite the fairy spirit or deva of the place to help you. As you become still, gently close your eyes and relax. Then in your mind's eye, surround yourself with love and life-giving light. As you sink into silence, feel yourself becoming light, almost transparent. Then in your mind's eye, begin to move like a fine mist over the land. Explore its every dip and curve. There's no need to hurry, as this is sacred business. Though it may be painful at times, do not shy away from the ravages you see before you. Take in the land's every hurt and scar. Then just as you think you know what needs to be done, go deeper. That way you will access the ancient dream for this place. The beauty is that when you take the time to work with the deva of the land, the plan you come up with will be far more complete than anything you could dream up on your own, because the deva has loved and tended this place for a very long time.

Once you have a clear sense of how to help heal the land, take heart because you're not doing this precious work on your own. The fairies are here with you, weaving their healing touches into the living fabric of the place. As you help repair the land, you might like to bless the earth for all it has brought you in the past and will again in the future. Then as you plant trees and tend the soil, hold your dream of the land perfectly restored in your heart as you work.

As you give the land your love, it will feed the soul of the place in return. Pay close attention to every little detail while you work. Give your time here your full and loving attention; then as you help heal the earth, notice how something inside you is also set free.

Once your work is done, it's good to celebrate all you've achieved with the help of the fairies. You may like to gather up some stones, crystals or other treasures to honour the spirit of the land. Find somewhere out of view to place your gifts of love, so your offering may add to the sacredness of this place.

You were always part of the dream for this land.
It has been waiting for your loving
touch for a very long time.

As you help restore the earth your very cells begin to sing, as you realise that your journey here is no accident. You were always part of the dream for this land. It has been waiting for your healing touch for a very long time.

OFTEN WE SEE FAIRY WORK AS MAGICAL,
AND ON ONE LEVEL IT IS.
BUT IN TRUTH, WHATEVER FAIRIES DO
SIMPLY FOLLOWS THE LAWS OF LIFE.
FAIRY FOLK THRIVE BECAUSE THEY UNDERSTAND
THE INTRICACIES OF DIVINE LAW,
AND HAPPILY WORK WITH THIS TO ACHIEVE ALL THEY DO.

Working with the Fairies

As I journeyed deeper into the world of the fairies, I was constantly amazed by the miracles that flowed from working closely with these remarkable beings. One of the most beautiful stories of such a partnership is that of George Washington Carver, born in Missouri. George rose above generations of slavery to become one of the greatest scientists of his time. As a boy, George had a profound relationship with nature. 'All the flowers talk to me and so do hundreds of little living things in the woods,' he explained. 'I learn by watching and loving everything.'[24]

While still a boy, George set up a garden in the woods, where he nurtured people's ailing plants. He also spent hours collecting plants from the woods to heal sick animals. This brilliant man spoke frequently of his relationship with the fairies and how they revealed some of nature's many secrets to him. 'When I touch that flower I am touching infinity,' he reflected. 'It existed long before there were human beings on this earth and will continue to exist for millions of years to come. Through the flower I talk to the Infinite, which is only a silent force. This is not a physical contact. It is not in the earthquake, wind or fire. It is in the invisible world. It is that still small voice that calls up the fairies.'[25]

When we fall out of reverence with nature and her fairy caretakers, we are out of balance.

Aware of the difficulties many southern farmers were facing with soils ruined by cotton, George devoted himself to finding a crop that could grow in poor soil, discovering peanuts could thrive there. Among his many achievements, we've got George Washington Carver to thank for is peanut butter! This highly respected college professor went on to discover how peanut oil can help restore limbs wasted by polio. Later he found over 300 uses for peanuts, including inks, soaps and shampoo. George Washington Carver also discovered 100 uses for sweet potatoes and 75 uses for pecans.

Working tirelessly with nature, he went on to create paper made from local pine trees, as well as face powders, printers' ink, wood stains and petroleum substitutes, to name but a few products. Many of his discoveries were taken up for manufacture, but such was George Washington Carver's respect for the fairies who had helped him with these breakthroughs, he rarely took out a patent on his work. His view was that God hadn't charged him for the raw materials, so nor would he.

George Washington Carver's life holds a whisper of what's possible, if we're prepared to work with nature and her fairy caretakers. Who knows what solutions we could discover to climate change and the many other issues impacting our world, if we truly listened to what nature and her loving caretakers have to tell us?

Too often we try to tackle these challenges alone, making life a whole lot more complicated than it need be.

Through the flower I talk to the Infinite,
which is only a silent force.
This is not a physical contact. It is not
in the earthquake, wind or fire.
It is in the invisible world. It is that still
small voice that calls up the fairies.

GEORGE WASHINGTON CARVER[26]

Half a world away in Scotland during the sixties, Peter and Eileen Caddy, their three children and friend Dorothy Maclean were unemployed and living in a caravan park outside the seaside village of Findhorn. Peter decided to grow vegetables to help make ends meet. His chances of succeeding were slim, as the soil was sandy and dry, the location cold and windswept. The fact that Findhorn only had around 26 inches of rain a year didn't help either. Much to her surprise, Dorothy began to converse with the devas there, who showed her how to make the most of the poor soil and tricky location. Over time, 65 varieties of vegetables, 42 herbs and 21 types of fruit flourished in this unforgiving climate. Their 40-pound cabbages, plus roses that bloomed in the snow, attracted the attention of horticulturalists the world over!

As Dorothy continued to work with the devas at Findhorn, she discovered a great deal about these remarkable beings, who oversee the welfare of the many different species. At one stage, she was driven to distraction by a family of rats living under her annexe. Disliking rats but not wanting to harm them, Dorothy spoke with the deva in charge of rats, explaining she couldn't have them living under her accommodation. The rat deva assured Dorothy that for as long as she stayed in the annexe, the rats would live elsewhere, which they did. After four years, Dorothy moved to another location in Findhorn. The morning after her move, the young man who'd taken over her annexe sought her out. 'I don't know how you could stand living there,' he complained. 'The rats kept me awake all night.' Dorothy smiled, to be reminded of just how precisely the rats had kept their end of the bargain.

During those years, Dorothy was dismayed to find one of the well-fed Findhorn cats catching birds and mice, and anything else she could. Dorothy tried to talk to the cat about this, but she could see the blinkers coming down every time she tried to persuade the stubborn puss to change her ways. So yet again, Dorothy went into a deep meditation and made contact with the deva who cared for all cats. After explaining how the cat was killing everything in sight, Dorothy was surprised when the deva asked her if she was willing to take on the responsibility of caring for cats everywhere. Taken aback, Dorothy admitted this task was beyond her. The deva went on to explain that cats retained their hunting instinct, so that if ever they were abandoned they could survive. She also said that until we humans take better care of cats, they would continue to hunt.

One of the great hallmarks of such extraordinary people as George Washington Carver, Dorothy Maclean and others who venture deep into the fairy world, is their profound reverence for the earth, and their great love of the nature spirits. They know how much these other-worldly souls can teach us about the intricacies of creation, when we're ready to listen.

Upsetting the Fairies

Until I delved into the world of the fairies, I'd no idea how much difficulty we cause our fairy friends. When we tear up trees and rocks, and mine and pollute the earth, we make things so much harder for fairies to maintain the intricate balance of life. Even far less dramatic actions can also upset the fairies.

Recently, my friend Linda told of a healer who was surprised to see a small gnome walking in after a female client. The client, who had come for a healing session, was completely unaware of her fairy companion. Quickly sizing up the situation, the healer thought it best to see what the gnome wanted first, then attend to her client.

It turned out the gnome was really angry with the lady. He'd come to the healing session to represent all the nature spirits in her garden. Apparently, when the lady landscaped her garden, she'd intended to leave a wild patch for the fairies. But as time went by, she forgot about this and had started to tidy and weed that area. This upset the nature spirits no end. Embarrassed, the lady said she'd make amends. The gnome thanked the lady and healer, then went to leave. The lady offered to give the gnome a lift back but he declined, saying he'd find his own way home.

Too often we disrupt the natural world and it's fairy helpers, because we don't think.

The fallout from our thoughtlessness towards the fairy world is nothing new for teacher and healer, Catherine Morgan, of Littleton, Colorado.[27] Catherine has seen fairies for over two decades and, through her Tasaris Center, now works to help repair the damage we do to the fairies. Through her work, Catherine has a very real sense of the impact we're having on nature and her fairy caretakers. Sometimes this harm happens in unexpected ways.

'When I trained in healing touch I was drawn to the woods, where I met a deva. It asked me to go to the nearby Platt River, which I did with two healer friends,' explains Catherine. 'There we came across a water sprite, who'd been trapped in the energetic field between two boulders. The boulders had been placed in the river for kayakers. While this might have seemed like a good idea, the energetic field around each stone acted like a net, which had then trapped the water sprite. Using all our skills (mine, my angel helpers and my friend with her reiki), we were able to release the water sprite. We needed to heal the stones too. They were lost and angry, because they hadn't been asked if they wanted to be placed in the river.'

Catherine related this incident to help me see just how much damage was caused by simply moving a couple of boulders. Over the years, I've moved things around in nature without a second thought. How often have I disturbed the delicate balance of life,

I wonder? And how much more harm do we do when we bull-doze whole tracts of land, ripping up rocks and trees, and building wherever we choose? Catherine is in no doubt about the some-times devastating impact. 'I have met many angry, grieving and lost fairies,' she tells.

In her delicate work, Catherine has found it's not just large constructions that can harm fairies. At one stage, she discovered a fairy trapped under the concrete in her driveway. He'd been caught there some years before, when the concrete was poured. Well used to rescuing these other-worldly beings, Catherine knew what was needed. 'We now know you can adjust your atoms, so you can move through solid objects,' she explains. 'When I saw the fairy under the concrete, I visualised the concrete as porous, so he could rise through the concrete. He was so thrilled to be free. He's now taken up residence in a neighbourhood tree.'

When life rewards us, often we are asked to give up something precious in return, as it's important to give as well as receive.

When we meddle with the laws of life, everything is turned upside down. Fairy tales are full of examples of humans causing chaos, because they don't understand just how intricate the fabric of life is. One of the many ways things come unstuck is when we fail to keep our end of the bargain.

In the timeless tale of Rumpelstiltskin, a miller lies to the king by saying his daughter can spin straw into gold. Delighted, the king asks the girl to do just that. Not surprisingly, the poor girl is out of her mind with fear about what will happen when the king discovers her father has lied. Seeing the girl's distress, the little dwarf Rumpelstiltskin comes to her rescue, on condition the girl give him her firstborn child. The terrified girl readily agrees and Rumplestiltskin spins the straw into gold. Thrilled with the results, the king marries the girl. But when her first child is born, she refuses to honour her promise and everything goes awry. While few of us would want to give away a child, the girl readily promised to do this. Rumplestiltskin kept his end of the bargain, only to be short-changed. No effort was made to compensate him in any way.

Why is it we find it so hard to honour our promises to the fairies? When life rewards us, we are often asked to give up something precious in return. This is an important principle, because receiving must be balanced by giving. Fairies know this universal law well, and live by this rule. They also know the magic available to those who tread lightly and wisely on earth. Sometimes we upset the balance, by trespassing into places in nature we're not meant to be. While we'd never think of barging into someone's house uninvited, we go wherever we like in the natural world, oblivious to the impact this has on the fairies and other creatures, large and small.

Those who live in tune with the earth have a different approach. Familiar with the places that are best left untouched, they respect these locations and make sure they're off limits, so as not to upset their balance. There are numerous ways we disrupt the harmony of a place, from disturbing a bird's nest or spider web, to contaminating a place with our chatter and emotional baggage.

International teacher, Alberto Villoldo, relates a fascinating experience he had some years back, while visiting two shamans in the Amazon. At one point, the shamans suggested Alberto cross a grassy area bordering the jungle. As Alberto walked across the clearing, the air was full of the sounds of creatures living in the jungle, but as soon as he stepped into the jungle everything became deathly quiet. Alberto assumed this silence was because these creatures could smell his deodorant or athlete's foot powder. The shamans suggested otherwise. Convinced he was right, Alberto covered himself in the boa constrictor fat left over from cooking and re-entered the jungle, only to have the monkeys and parrots and all the other creatures there fall silent once again. Shocked by this, Alberto began to see just how far he was from a close relationship with nature. After a great deal of reflection, he realised that whole parts of him had come adrift from the natural world.

It took him a few years to come into a genuine sense of oneness with creation. 'Ten years later, after I had learned the ways of the Earthkeepers, I found that when I would stride into the rainforest, the creatures and insects who sensed my presence would recognise me as someone who lived in the garden, and their chattering and squawking and singing would continue uninterrupted,' he reflects. 'They knew I was someone who walked with beauty on the earth, who belonged to them.'[28] Isn't this just the most astonishing experience? It holds so many precious insights.

So how can you and I walk more lightly on the earth? How can we discern which places are best left to the fairies? At first these locations may be difficult to spot, as we're all so busy and move around a lot. In turn, this makes it hard for the land and its fairy keepers to communicate with us. Yet as Mother Earth continues to struggle, it's vital we make life easier for fairies by slowing down a bit and thinking about our actions, by being more open and more observant to the nuances around us. It's interesting to see what happens when we do cross the line, even unintentionally, and venture into places we're clearly not meant to be.

It was really strange. This little figure wasn't human.
He was from a different kingdom.
He was like a gnome you'd see in storybooks.

Sue has a great love and respect for nature. She was on a night walk in a national park, hoping to contact fairies, when she had an experience she hadn't bargained on. 'We'd been going for quite a while when I noticed this little shrub,' she explains. 'I could suddenly see what looked like a man. He was quite a hairy, bulky figure like a gnome. I thought to myself, "What's that?" As I asked the question, an unspoken conversation began between us. "Come and follow me," the little gnome demanded. I didn't want to go with him. "Now you've seen me, you've got to come now," he insisted. But I didn't want to go, because I didn't know where he wanted to take me. It was really strange. This little figure wasn't human. He was from a different kingdom. He was like a gnome you'd see in storybooks.

'He had his hand out, as he was communicating with me. When I refused to go with him, a huge lightning bolt shot out of his hand. My two friends saw it as well. It was just as you see lightning in the sky, when it rains and storms. The lightning bolt hit my leg. I couldn't move, and couldn't walk on my leg for three days. It was a really strong pain, an odd pain, not a pain I'd known before. I was concerned as to whether or not I'd get my leg working again. When I got home, I was searching around for friends who could do a reiki treatment on me, because I didn't feel I could go to the doctor.'

Luckily, Sue did come right. Sue is very respectful of nature, but as this incident shows, there's so much about the fairy realms we still don't get. Sue made a good call not to go with this other-worldly stranger, as she didn't feel good about it.

Mama has a German background and now lives in the Pacific Islands. She also had an unusual fairy encounter that gave her cause to pause. Late one afternoon while she and her husband were staying in a cottage, Mama decided to go for a stroll. On her walk she had 'an almost electric feeling'. The hairs on her arms 'literally stood on end'. When Mama glanced in the direction of this feeling, she noticed an area of 'brilliant green sword grass' under a clutch of trees. In among this grass were many 'emerald green' fairies with long rather 'misty-looking bodies', and almost human-looking faces with tan 'skin'. 'They were making very high-pitched noises that sounded like they were calling to me. They floated above the ground in a sort of undulating kind of way, like grass blowing in the breeze. I had this urge to go there, but for some reason kept walking.'[29]

Who knows what may have happened to Sue or Mama had they gone with the fairies? They may have been perfectly fine, or may have been in trouble. When we venture into the world of nature spirits, it's like wandering into an unfamiliar part of town. We need to make wise choices and behave in a low-key manner, so we can pick up on whether this is where we're meant to be.

They were making very high-pitched noises that
sounded like they were calling to me.
They floated above the ground in a sort
of undulating kind of way,
like grass blowing in the breeze.

MAMA

Celia has had many fairy encounters, each teaching her a little more of this enchanting other world. She was walking in the Snowy Mountains in Australia, when she and her friends came across a few rocks shaped like easychairs. It looked like the perfect place to take a break. Celia insists she wasn't thinking of fairies at the time. 'We had walked for hours and felt the need to sit down on those inviting rocks,' she recalls. 'In my half-asleep state, I suddenly felt like someone was kicking my right calf. I became aware of a small woolly creature, completely covered by thick, long strands of fur. He was just tall enough to come up to my knees, and angrily told me to get off his stone, as I was blocking the entrance to his home. Only after excusing myself and promising to leave the seat soon, did the offended goblin calm down. We became almost friends. He complained that we humans were all too noisy, disturbing the living beings in the flower-bedecked meadows. I could only agree, thinking of our incessant chatter.'

Sometimes the anger fairies show towards us goes deeper. At one stage, Robert Ogilvie Crombie (Roc), who we met earlier, was on the Black Isle in Scotland with Peter Caddy from Findhorn. During their stay, they visited a fairy glen Roc loved as a small child. To Roc's dismay, the glen was overgrown. The overall feel of the place was dark and dispiriting. Two elfin figures appeared, warning Roc to leave at once. Shocked by their hostility, Roc explained that he knew Pan and other nature spirits. On hearing this, their anger abated.

Roc was invited to return alone that evening, which he did. Venturing with these fairy figures deep into the glen, Roc realised the elves weren't so much angry as distraught. When Roc met their leader, he was hostile at first too. 'You upset the balance of nature, destroy the animals, turn land to desert, cut and burn the large trees, maim the landscape by blasting great wounds in the hills and mountains, and slashing the living earth so that it will not heal,' this forbidding figure told him. 'It was once beautiful. Can you blame us if we consider you a parasite on the face of the earth?' Roc tried to explain that humans were making more of an effort. Accepting this, their leader went on to explain how hard the elves worked with the life force of each plant to help them grow. [30]

Like the fairies, you and I are caretakers of our tiny planet. Taking proper care of the earth sometimes requires us to make sacrifices for the greater good. A few decades ago, the people of Ballymagroarty Scotch in Ireland were distressed to discover a precious fairy tree they'd nurtured for generations was to be cut down to make way for a new road. Though it was good money, the contractors were nervous about undertaking the project. They'd grown up with stories of fairies and knew of their delicate relationship with the land. Aware of what was at stake, they refused to cut the tree down, and so the road was rerouted.

To some, this may seem like a foolish decision. But there's nothing naive about honouring the intricate web of life, and walking the world with wisdom and grace.

Unusual Characters

The more you discover about fairies, the more you start to see things from their point of view. You also realise that while you may wish desperately to see a fairy or two, not all fairies want this. Many fairies don't like humans, because we're loud and self-absorbed. Some fairies are simply unused to humans. Others are frightened by how destructive we are.

There are times we humans are terrified by the fairies we glimpse, because they don't look as we imagined. This doesn't necessarily mean the fairy is sinister, so much as not what was expected. The fright you have when you see a strange-looking fairy is similar to catching sight of a spider out of the blue. It gives you a momentary start.

So if you see a fairy which looks a bit scary, don't panic. Tune into your intuition to size them up, to help you decide whether this fairy simply looks a bit weird or is out to hurt you in some way.

There are fairies who, like some humans,
have forgotten who they are and what they came here to do.

After immersing herself in a fairy book, Brenda was really keen to see fairies. She'd read that to invite fairies into your house you should put dried rosemary on the windowsills, which she did. Late one night as she was passing the kitchen window, she caught sight of something out of the corner of her eye. Looking out of the window there was a light green figure with black hair and 'moth-like wings'. This little figure was about four inches high and stared back at Brenda with beady eyes. Terrified by this strange figure, Brenda didn't sleep for days, because the fairy 'did not look pretty like in fairy pictures, but rather scary looking.'[31]

There are many different ways fairies can appear before you, often looking like nothing you've seen before, but this doesn't automatically mean they're dark or dangerous. As you journey deeper into the fairy realm, you discover countless species of fairies, from simple little beings to highly evolved fairies such as devas. As we've already seen, fairies often appear to you in the forms you expect, so you can recognise them. As fairies become more familiar to you, you may start to see them in less familiar forms.

Molly, a medical professional who travels the world teaching medical staff, has seen fairies since being a small child. As her relationship with fairies developed, so too have the ways in which they reveal themselves. 'When I was really really little, we had an oak tree in our backyard. Dad put a swing in the tree. As I'd be playing on the swing, the fairies would be flying all around me,' she tells. 'But whenever grown-ups appeared, they'd disappear really quickly. At this age, they looked like transparent little specs of light, like sparkles on water. If I looked at them through my peripheral vision, I could see their body shapes and they were all different. They'd buzz around really quickly. They looked like little people.'

Molly continued: 'Then I stopped seeing fairies at eight or nine. I was still aware of them and could feel them around me as a teenager. I could make out different fairies. Some had a light energy, some a deep wise energy, but I couldn't see anything. Then I grew up and did lots of things. I got very cross that they wouldn't show themselves to me any more. I told them to be serious about showing themselves to me or not to bother, as I was serious about communicating with them. That's when everything changed. I saw all sorts of fairies. Some had long faces and noses and big pointy lips. Some had legs like people, but frog's feet. Some had wings like dragonflies or butterflies. Some had tiny wings. Others had humungous wings. Some didn't have wings. They were just as different as we are.'

Like every life form, each fairy has its own role and habitat. That's why fairies often take on the look of the landscape where they live. Sometimes they may look a bit weird to us, but it makes good sense that they blend in with their surroundings, as Lucille discovered when she was out deep in the Australian desert. 'I was in the Bungle Bungle Range, where they have the lovely deep red brown honeycomb rock,' she explains. 'I was there on a special trip. We stayed with the Aboriginal people on their land. While I was there, I saw little people. There were hundreds of them marching in line. The local people know all about them and said these were the keepers of the land. They were the same colour as the landscape, but in little people form. They were like the fairies of that area.'

As fairies are committed to their work in nature, it's no surprise they take on the appearance of a place, or of the rocks, trees, grasses or shrubs they care for. Fairies come in all shapes and sizes. If you want to get closer to them it helps to have an open mind, as Bob Crombie who takes night walks in nature knows well. 'On one night walk, there was this big being about eight feet tall just watching us,' he tells. 'Your hair begins to stand on end when you see beings like this. It started to follow us. This being regularly follows us when we do the walk. It puts the wind up you like you wouldn't believe. It's a terrific part of the night walk, because fear takes you places. Fear makes you let go and pay attention like you wouldn't believe. It helps you make a shift, and takes you into places of incredible peace and beauty. That's why I never worry about the fear, as it's incredibly beneficial.'

Bob is no novice in the fairy realms. His is a lifetime's commitment to nature. Unlike most, Bob knows how to walk harmlessly in fairy places, and protect himself when he's in unexpected situations.

I saw little people. There were hundreds of them marching in line. They were the same colour as the landscape, but in little people form.

LUCILLE

The ability to enter fairy places without harming anything, and to know how to handle yourself when you are there, is an essential part of making contact, because tricky situations can occur. 'Another time I was out walking with my nephew in his twenties, who was needing to sort a few things out,' Bob explains. 'We had an interesting night and were in that state of heightened awareness. We were on the way out, when my nephew suddenly grabbed my arm. All I was aware of was this terrible pressure on my arm. Then when I looked up about thirty or so yards away, there was this gigantic big black hulk of a figure. It was about eight feet tall and humanoid in appearance, but you couldn't see any features. I didn't get a chance to do anything much, because my nephew started to panic. He was shouting and waving the figure away. I kept saying to him, "Don't! Don't!" But I couldn't stop him.

'This being didn't like my nephew's fear and defensive reaction. I knew the thing to do was not to react with fear, but to project good feelings—love and peace and harmony. It came towards us quite fast. My nephew was yelling and hanging onto me, then he gave out this tremendous yell and took off. Meanwhile, this thing came straight at me and just picked me up and threw me. I flew through the air and landed in this great big bush and came down laughing my head off. I had no fear, but was awestruck and delighted by what had happened. This being just stopped and looked at me, then walked away. It matched the descriptions of a yowie. You see lots of them up there. A lot of people catch sight of them at a distance in certain places. They seem to have certain pathways they use back and forth. It's interesting. It's like there's a whole ecology in the other world, as much as there is in our world. You just don't find certain species of fairies anywhere. They have specific places where they go and live. Their world has a distribution of beings, as do we.'

Lucille, now a grandmother, has seen other out-of-the-ordinary fairy figures and wasn't phased by them, though she would have found it hard to physically protect herself had they challenged her. Like Bob, she's spent a lifetime committed to nature, and she's a healer too. She knows how to read situations, and the importance of love and respect. 'I've seen the bunyip or yowie,' she tells. 'It's a big and hairy-like person—huge, about forty feet high, like a tree in size. I didn't worry about it. It was where they live. When you have these experiences there must be no fear, just love.' This is not the only giant being Lucille has come across. 'When I went on the night walk, I saw tall people. They might be the keepers of the land. They were from a different realm. They were about five feet tall. They had different kinds of faces, human bodies and animal faces. I wasn't afraid of them. They were just different.'

Scientist Penny Kelly, who now runs a vineyard with her husband, also enjoys a very special relationship with the fairies at her vineyard. The fairy folk who live there have taught her much about life, which she has written about in detail in *The Elves of Lily Hill Farm*. Penny captures her delight when first glimpsing fairies beautifully. 'Suddenly I realised that for the first time I was seeing them!' she tells. 'They were short, perhaps two feet tall, with an assortment of baggy clothes and hats. A few of them carried sticks or some kind of handled instruments, and all of them looked aged and ageless.'[32]

As we delve deeper into nature, some are privileged to have direct encounters with the mighty figure of Pan, who oversees the natural world. Often these encounters are deeply moving, a powerful reminder that we are forever connected to nature. At the beginning of an amazing series of experiences, teacher Michael Roads met Pan. While he didn't recognise this timeless figure at first, Michael was immediately drawn to his 'sensitivity' and 'strength', and to his face which he describes as 'fierce yet gentle, mellow yet wild and free'. So began an extraordinary friendship, which Michael describes beautifully: 'Pan looks at me and smiles, and within that smile is more love than I ever knew was possible. Love beyond human comprehension washes over me, bathing me in sheer goodness,' he tells, adding, 'he is the violet-pink light, the energy of earth, the spirit of Nature.'[33]

Like many who journey deep into the fairy realms, Penny Kelly finally meets Pan as well. He introduces himself as Harvey. 'Facing me was a tall slender man, casually leaning with his elbow on one of the end posts,' she explains. 'He had on a flannel shirt which was tucked neatly into a pair of jeans, and he wore a straw hat. His fingers were long and slim and his face seemed young, but he struck me as unimaginably old. Most shocking of all though, there seemed to be horns on his head under the hat, and he did not have feet—he had hooves!' [34] As Penny worked more closely with nature, Pan was there helping guide her so she could begin to see the bigger picture, and get a greater sense of what's possible when you work with the fairy kingdom.

All these experiences and more help you begin to appreciate some of the many beings who inhabit the fairy world, showing us how intricate and complex the fairy realms are. Overseeing the fairies and reflecting the divine plan for creation is Pan himself. Sadly, he has been demonised. Tragically, the being whose job it is to support the whole of creation has been cast as devilish, as something to hate and fear. Alongside this fearful attitude towards Pan has come our separation from creation and much destruction of the earth.

Fallen Fairies

It's important to understand that not all fairies are full of sweetness and light. There are fairies who, like some humans, have forgotten who they are and what they came here to do. Instead of infusing life with their beauty and nurture, fallen fairies bring hurt, confusion and pain into the world.

Lisa, who sees fairies, agrees that not all fairies are good or kind. She can tell what a fairy is like by their eyes. 'You can sense their hearts by their eyes, as you can with humans,' she explains. 'If they have a dark soul, their eyes will be "dark".' The first fairy Lisa saw, which she now thinks was a brownie, had 'pure innocent eyes', reminding her of the photos of saints she's familiar with. When she thinks back to her first fairy encounter, Lisa recalls the fairy's 'soft and unselfish' eyes, and that the fairy 'was thinking only of me and not of herself'. Lisa believes bad or fallen fairies are the way they are, because they have let 'hate enter their hearts.'

Before we get too paranoid about bad fairies, Lisa also reminds us that many humans live in the same dark space. 'We humans really can be repulsive towards this earth and environment,' she points out. 'And they (the fairies) see all the rotten things we do, like greedily destroying their woodlands and clubbing baby seals to death.'[35] Lisa's response to dark fairies is to pray for them, hoping this may 'plant a spark' and soften their hearts.

So when you venture into the fairy realms, do so with a pure heart. It's also vital you do so with your eyes wide open, including your intuitive third eye. Prepare yourself, as you would for any spiritual journey. Begin by visualising yourself surrounded by the pure golden light of divine being. Be clear in your heart about why you'd like to make contact, then see what happens as you start to immerse yourself in nature. Should you find yourself in a difficult situation, you can call on beings of profound love, for assistance, on your power animal, or other sources for good and protection you already work with. When you do begin your journey into the fairy world, tread wisely, carefully and respectfully. Don't judge every fairy you meet simply by how they appear. Learn to look into their eyes and their hearts.

Almost all those I've spoken to had nothing but uplifting experiences when with fairies. However some have encountered dark figures and places. Celia remembers going with teacher, Miss Peters, on a class outing to a meadow surrounded by a thicket of trees. After a pleasant lunch on the grass, Celia felt what she describes as 'a strong indescribable urge' to enter the forest. 'My first impression was an unexpected darkness and the smell of dampness,' she recalls. 'A strange, gloomy feeling crept into my soul, as soon as I was confronted by prickly bushes under sunless, dark trees. The thick vegetation hardly allowed me to advance. I looked around in vain for a path. The trunks of the trees stood closely together. The ground was uneven, with large stones and creepers which seemed to throw out their arms to strangle me. The more I walked, the denser and darker the forest appeared. It seemed like a world of an unknown dread, far removed from the sunlight of the meadow. The voices of the other children faded quickly and I was aware of being alone.'

It was hardly taller than I was. It was
clothed in a black cloak,
the hood pulled over the face—if there was a face.

CELIA

'I had the feeling there was someone trying to pull me back. Fear overcame me, so I looked behind me. There, half hiding behind a large tree, stood a black figure. I could not make out what it was, but knew that it was neither child, nor teacher, nor any grown-up. It was hardly taller than I was. It was clothed in a black cloak, the hood pulled over the face—if there was a face. Now the black thing was advancing towards me. I turned around to run away, but thorny bushes held me back. I tripped over some stones and was lying helplessly on the ground for a moment. Injuring my hands, I pushed myself up and could run again. I did not dare look back, but felt the fearsome mysterious creature coming ever closer.

'Suddenly, it was touching me. I was forced to turn around and look. What a profound shock to my whole being. It had no face. For a moment we both stared at each other, as if bewitched. Then it moved with such speed, disappearing sideways in the thickets. As if released from a spell, I ran towards the clearing. I just had to get away from this inexplicable freakish sight. I did not know how, but all at once I found myself on the grass in the middle of all the boys and girls, playing happily with balls and skipping ropes. No-one had noticed my absence. I could not possibly tell them about my experience in the woods, as I lacked the words to describe what I had seen. I was still trembling. "Don't be shy, join us!" the children called out, encouraging me to join in their games.'

When Sue was on a night walk with her friend Bob, she also had an experience which shook her up. 'There was a being showed up who was very, very tall, maybe about seven feet tall,' she recalls. 'We were in our vehicle at the time and this figure was standing outside. Bob had seen him before and knew about him. He looked a bit like a human, but more like a yeti. I could feel him. He was looking at us. We were in his space, so I wasn't going to get out of the car. Looking back, he wasn't happy at us being there. It was a different feeling to the light of the fairies with their blissful, friendly energy I'd encountered earlier that night. The contrast was very interesting. What I sense is that some fairies have a real sense of joy and freedom; others easily scare people, because they are frightening. I think there's definitely an evolution going on among the fairies. There's more than one kingdom in the fairy realm. The kingdoms are vast and never-ending.'

There was a being showed up who was very very tall ...
Looking back, he wasn't happy at us being there.
It was a different feel to the light of the fairies
with their blissful friendly energy I'd encountered earlier.

SUE

When Jay was sixteen he went camping with friends and had a terrifying experience while out filming for a web page they were working on. As darkness fell, Jay decided to go for a walk. Night closed in suddenly and he realised he was lost. It was then he heard footsteps a few paces behind him. Turning, he saw what he describes as a male figure dressed in black. It moved towards him and in a low voice said it was going to take Jay back to its lair in the mountains, eat his flesh and see what his 'body was made of'. Jay was paralysed with fear, as he watched the figure come closer. He wanted to take to his heels, but found himself rooted to the spot. Jay could see its red face, long nose and bushy eyebrows. When this sinister figure spoke, he did so without moving his lips.

Then Jay heard his friends calling out for him and turned to see where they were. The next instant he looked back, to find the terrifying figure had disappeared. When Jay told his friends what had happened, they didn't believe him. Later that night, when everyone was asleep, Jay woke to the sound of footsteps. Curled up in the foetal position, he closed his eyes tight, not daring to move. The whispering started all over again. The figure told Jay it would by back when he was alone. Jay survived the experience but, needless to say, he's never been back to that location.[36]

Whenever you encounter fairies it's important you do so with caution, as your ignorance about this vast realm can make you vulnerable. 'There are dark fairies,' Molly, a medical professional, affirms. 'A few years ago I had an accident, where I fell down the stairs and broke my back. I was on a lot of medication and so my defences were low. I was depressed with all the pain, because I could hardly walk. I was like that for three years. When I was in my very low period, these ugly fairy beings would come to me, often at night. There was this black horrible being, like how I'd expect a banshee to look. It had long, bony, horrible fingers and looked really skeletal. Sometimes I'd wake up and it'd be on my face, like it was trying to squash the life out of me.

'Every time I'd try to build up my positive energy, but I wasn't able to connect with the light. It was like someone falling into a lake. The more I struggled, the worse it got. I needed to be saved by someone from the shore. When my friend Sue walked into the room, she 'saw' hundreds of black hairy spiders on the ceiling, dropping onto my bed. It took all her healing, and the use of special healing symbols only used when people are really under threat, to turn things around. She worked on me for four hours. Then she'd come back each day. There's a lot of negative or evil energy, as well as the good stuff, in the fairy realm. It's important to be very selective about engaging with other-worldly beings. You can't have light without the darkness.'

So should you seek to enter the fairy realms, make sure you do so with protection, wisdom and light. Know that not all beautiful fairies have your best interests at heart, and not all strange-looking fairies are harmful.

THE FAIRIES GAVE ME NO WARNING, EXCEPT THIS
GRADUAL INCREASE IN MY AWARENESS OF BEAUTY,
AS THEY WORKED SUBLIMINALLY ON MY MIND AND SOUL
TO LIBERATE MY SENSES FROM THE
TYRANNY OF THAT UNFELT FEAR.[37]

Vivienne Manouge

Wounded Spirit

In earlier times, people called on the joy and wisdom of the fairies to help them thrive and live in greater balance with life. Now with mass-produced farming, food often lacks nutrients, as we no longer allow the earth to rest and replenish. At the same time, the complex chemistry behind genetically modified foods places our bodies under pressure. While our food may look good, it frequently lacks real goodness, so our health is compromised.

The way many people live on the planet is a little like a child let loose in a candy store. Treading in places we know little about, we frequently cause ourselves and others harm. These days, we take such plants as cacao (cocoa), corn and tobacco without thought, unaware that these plants are considered sacred. Our carelessness comes at a high price, causing us to suffer addictions and ill-health.

For generations, native peoples have treasured tobacco and used it to communicate with the spirit world. The gifting and smoking of tobacco was a sacred process. Elders would announce their holy intentions, as they lit the tobacco to activate its sacred possibilities. Tobacco was always given as an offering to the plant world, before medicinal plants were picked. Now tobacco is a multi-billion dollar industry and is used indiscriminately by billions, to chill out and de-stress. More often than not, people become addicted to tobacco—such is their need for this sacred plant. I sometimes wonder whether at a deeper level, those addicted to cigarettes are hungry for the sacred potential of this plant? Without the knowledge and reverence for what they're doing, they're left with a longing that can never be fulfilled, risking lung cancer in the process.

Corn is also revered by native peoples, as a means of sustaining life. In some creation myths, the first man and woman were formed by white and yellow corn. When someone was very ill, the Mayans would feed them a diet of corn to help restore their health. Across the Americas, the 'hair' of the corn also had many healing properties, ranging from asissting with constipation, diarrhoea, urinary retention and bladder infection to infertility and period pains, as well as strengthening the womb after childbirth.[38]

Cacao is known to create a deep sense of wellbeing in those who take it. In ancient times, cacao was used to help those who had lost weight to regain their robustness and to stimulate the nervous system, digestion and elimination.[39] When used for sacred purposes, cacao was said to unlock the secrets of the soul. Who would have thought the key ingredient of chocolate could have such potent possibilities?

As we contemplate the depth of healing these plants offer, we realise we're touching on something profound. It's hard to fully recognise how much good we can bring to the world when we start to comprehend how sacred plant life really is. All too frequently, we grasp at things we don't quite understand, destroying our equilibrium and nature's harmony in the process. Sadly, the results of our blindness are all around us. Our world is now reeling from the effects of smoking, from the harmful levels of corn syrup in foods and much more besides. Yet it need not be this way. When we return to a place of balance and reverence, everything changes. When we're wiser, humbler and more discerning, we're more willing to make good choices, instead of those based purely on advantage or profit. Living in harmony with nature and her fairy caretakers offers us a way back.

It's no accident that our precious earth is suffering so much at present. No longer do we nurture her or give her our love. We're too busy, too self-absorbed. But as saddening as this is, the fairies are quick to remind us that what is wounded can be healed. They also gently remind us that we cannot fully heal the earth, until we are whole too. To return to balance, we need time for quiet, to be around those who feed our soul, to breathe in the fresh air, to feel the precious earth beneath our feet. These and other life-enhancing steps are significant, because they reconnect us to all that is, reminding us how good it is to be alive.

Fairies freely offer us their healing radiance. They work hard to help mend those bits of us that are broken. They inspire us, make us feel more hopeful, assisting us to find joy in simple things. These gifts are profound, because they infuse our bodies with life-giving light. The more light you and I embody, the lighter we become, making it easier for us to laugh, sing and dance, to be 100 percent alive. When we're full of life, it's so much easier to bring love and hope to those who feel loveless or despairing, to embrace the promise in each moment, and rid ourselves of all those things that hold us back.

Fairies help us reconnect with ourselves and our world, by helping interest us in nature, in our homes and gardens, in beauty and creativity. Some fairies also take a close interest in our well-being and assist the flow of life through our bodies. Medical intuitive, Karen Swain told me how she discovered this, after attending a talk by British healer, Lorna Todd. During her talk, Lorna explained that just as nature has a fairy attending every blade of grass, there's also a tiny fairy assigned to each and every cell in our body. These miniscule fairies make sure each cell is functioning and is properly connected to every other cell. Lorna's talk on the fairy caretakers tending our bodies had a profound effect on Karen.

As clear as day, I could see beautiful sparkling
lights very close to the corners of my eyes.
They stayed with me for some time, as if
reminding me of their presence.

KAREN

'That night, when I returned home and was undressing, I was thinking about the support we get from the nature spirits and their infinite supply of love and nourishment, when I noticed brilliant sparkling tubes of white light out of the corners of both eyes,' Karen explains. 'As I turned my head to see what was happening, they disappeared. I'd never experienced light like this. I thought I might be imagining it, but as my attention returned to undressing, it happened again. As clear as day, I could see beautiful sparkling lights very close to the corners of my eyes. This time I didn't turn my head to look directly at them. They stayed with me for some time, as if contentedly reminding me of their presence. Their radiance was like the light around Tinkerbell in *Peter Pan*. Their presence seemed to be connected to the attention I was giving my body. This, I imagined, was their way of telling me they are always present, caring for my body.

'Having these beautiful lights so close was and is a huge comfort,' Karen continues. 'Knowing that the devic realm is working tirelessly to support me is very reassuring in times of uncertainty. I now know that when I become overly concerned about health or money, I have an ever-present realm of energy working to restore my life back to harmonious balance. I can relax and let the universe handle the details, just as it is always doing in the beat of my heart and the rush of blood that supplies my body, and in the way my body repairs itself when I cut or damage it.

'I am not in control of these things, but some form of creation is there being of service to me. There is an intelligence in nature that is helped by the devic kingdom. This intelligence creates life effortlessly, just as the beauty of nature is created effortlessly. I think we can all take this lesson from nature, that creating a beautiful life is effortless. I now see these beautiful lights often, usually when I am thinking or talking about my body or some facet of healing. Their presence reminds me I am never alone, and that the universe is always looking after me.'

Karen's beautiful account allows us to glimpse how much more there is to the world of fairies. But what is this light that Karen saw in and around the fairies, and how can we access it? Ultimately light is life. Light is love also. These three qualities are inextricably connected. So when you experience a fairy's radiance, you're also experiencing life-giving energy and love. This is the magic fairies work with constantly. It's the very same magic you have at your fingertips.

When your love/light shines strong, it helps people feel safe and nurtured, and the whole of creation to flourish. Basically, the more powerful your love/light, the more every living thing is elevated by your presence. Just to see or hear from you is balm to another's soul.

So why not learn from the fairies? Make a habit of filling yourself with life-giving love and radiance. You can achieve this by surrounding yourself with people and situations which feed you. Then, as you become wiser and more loving, you're more at one with life.

A Little Wildness

There are so many ways you can be at one with life. Your soul's longings often provide the key. Do you ever long to be out in nature, to feel the sun on your face and the wind in your hair? Nature feeds us and frees us. It can heal us as well. Whenever you connect with nature and her fairy helpers, you're taking part in a holy act that helps bring you back to wholeness. So start to listen more closely to your longings to be in nature. Make time to lie on the earth, to breathe in fresh mountain air, to walk in the woods, to stare up at the crescent moon. Note how you're subtly transformed by such experiences.

One of the most beautiful ways to help achieve this is to leave a little room inside for the wild part of you to thrive, as the wild part of you is truly breathtaking. It's that part of you that's powerful and pure and gentle, and forever connected to the web of life. Your wild self is not afraid to seek out what works for you.

It's never imprisoned by what others think or say. It encourages you to open your eyes and delve deep into your heart.

It's from your wild self that much inspiration comes, and through the wild part of you that you can reclaim the wisdom and innocence you were born with. So treasure and nurture your wild self, as it's your divine compass. It helps you walk authentically, joyously and harmlessly on the earth. It's through your wild self that you'll find much of the freedom you ache for. Your wild essence is always there for you.

So when next you feel a bit sad, lonely or lacking in creativity, all you need do is simply retreat into your own inner wilderness. Allow it to warm those parts of you that feel lost, abandoned or empty.

As you get to know your wild self, your priorities shift and it becomes the most natural thing in the world to seek out wilderness places. Suddenly, you're surprised to find yourself aching for wild spaces. Sometimes this longing will be so intense that you'll feel like you could die without access to nature. Don't ever be concerned by this. Be excited, because your wild self knows that it's in these pristine environments that hope, healing and clarity are found. That's why so many great spiritual figures through the ages have spent time in the wilderness. When all distractions are stripped away, these places connect you powerfully with the divine. It's also where the fairies live and thrive.

When you spend time in wilderness places, you get to see and experience yourself in new ways and witness many tiny miracles. Just to see the frost paint the world white, or to catch a dewdrop on a blade of grass is enough to make your soul sing. At first, you may feel a little intimidated about the thought of the wilderness. I know I did until I got out there. Then everything changed; I felt like I'd come home. The relief and beauty of being in these

216

pristine places is huge and hard to put into words, other than wilderness moments are forever imprinted on your soul.

Things changed dramatically for Sarah, a young city executive, when she took a short break in a remote location. Once she and her partner had settled into their wilderness retreat, Sarah found she was able to connect to the land at a level she'd never expected. 'We started to take holidays in a remote little cottage that's in the middle of nowhere,' she tells. 'And it was here I started to see fairies, especially in the cottage. The first time was when I had just got out of the shower and was drying myself off. I could see quite a lot of them around me. I can't describe them in words, but I did see them clearly enough. I remember the feeling they gave me was a pure, whole feeling. Though there were bad things happening at the time, it was like everything was going to be okay. We continued to go back to the cottage. My partner wasn't well, but every time we went back he got better and better. I didn't realise it then, but I was also getting stronger in myself.

'The cottage was the perfect environment. There was no TV, and no reception on our cell phones. We only ate really pure food there. We'd just go and sit with the trees, or climb the mountains, or sit by the lake. Early morning was when I saw the fairies. Time went really fast there. It was like really sped up. There were so many experiences. There was a lot of light and flickerings around me. After that first fairy experience, I saw fairies a lot. One day I just stood there and they were all around me, like whirlpools of light. I just looked at them in amazement, and then some time after they were gone. Then I started to experience them at home in the city.'

Having a handful of days in the wilderness can literally change your life. When you make the effort to get out into the wilds, even for a short time, you discover many powerful gifts there, that will stay with you in the weeks and months to come. 'I now realise the place we went to had healing properties in the earth as well. I'm sure that was partly because it was remote, untouched. There the trees spoke to us and had stories to tell. It kind of created a ripple effect. I really got in tune with trees,' explains Sarah. 'Even now I'm back in the city, when I go for walks in the morning I just feel each tree has its own life and personality. That time in the wilds helped get me into alignment with other living things.'

Knowing all you now do about fairies, this is the perfect time to explore your own wild self. While it may at first seem strange or a long way from your everyday self, there's nothing about the wild part of you to fear. You don't have to go on a survival trek. Just take yourself off to somewhere that is relatively untouched by human intervention. Somewhere that's calling you. Embrace and explore it. Allow it to touch the most authentic, inspired part of you. Then you'll see how your wild self helps you connect to yourself and others, to your dreams and to what you came here to do.

WHEREVER IS LOVE AND LOYALTY, GREAT
PURPOSES AND LOFTY SOULS,
EVEN THOUGH IN A HOVEL OR A MINE,
THERE IS FAIRY LAND.[40]

Charles Kingsley

Crossing Over

When I set out on this adventure, I hardly dared hope I'd meet people who'd crossed over into fairyland, but I did. One of these special people is mystic and ranger, Bob Crombie, who's also one of the most grounded, straight-talking individuals you'll ever meet. During night walks and other excursions in nature, Bob has ventured into the fairy realms on a number of occasions. A key part of this experience for Bob is knowing when he's reached the in-between, that magical space which bridges our world and that of the fairy.

One of the signs for Bob of an in-between place is when he's suddenly surrounded by mist. 'The mists are one of the dead giveaways you're in a threshold place, that you're ready to change your consciousness and move into another world,' he tells. 'The mists are a good indicator you're moving from one state to another. It's good to know this, because people aren't used to paying attention. Something can happen right in front of you, but you literally don't see it, because it's out of the normal.'

The mists are one of the dead giveaways
you're in a threshold place,
that you're ready to change your consciousness
and move into another world.
The mists are a good indicator you're
moving from one state to another.

BOB CROMBIE

'When people can see and recognise they're in 'other' places, they may see the mist around them, and how it's come up close and right around them,' Bob explains. 'They also see how the weather is suddenly very windy and cold. Then they realise you don't get mist when it's really windy. So when the mist comes up like this, something's about to happen. This mist travels up to about six feet high. That's why some sacred places are known as mist-filled places. It's a prelude to other worlds. I just love it when the mist comes up.'

Bob is one of the few people I've met who has ventured beyond the mists and into the fairy realms. 'When you get into the rainforest, the energy there seems take you to a place I call the mottled world,' he tells. 'Suddenly out of the darkness, the world will go all spotty and mottled, brownish-coloured and shimmery. Like the mist, it's another threshold and indicates I'm ready to go into yet another world.

'When we get into the mottled world, there's another world we reach, which is the silver world. You are right through when you reach the silver world. You're in another place. You're actually there. It's just the most amazing place. Sometimes when we do the night walks, it's so dark you can't see the hand in front of your face. You're walking down feeling your way with your feet and suddenly you can see. Everything is all silver and so beautiful. You feel quite different. There's this amazing sense of wellbeing and excitement. The silver world looks very similar to our world. You can see here. Everything's lit by a silvery light. There's still colour, but everything's lit with silver.'

It's fascinating to discover there's a sense of progression from one world to the next in the fairy realm, yet to know you're still in the same location.

Lucille is a grandmother and healer, who's been out with Bob on night walks. She has experienced this silvern world too. 'Even though it was pitch dark, the trees were all lit up like they had a spotlight on them,' she recalls. 'Then we went into another area where there were all these bushes, just ordinary bushes, but they had like fairy lights on them. You'd come up to them and they'd go off. Then the lights would go on again. In another area I knew well, it was like going into a disco. There were so many lights, just white lights. It was joyous, like a celebration. The drawings we see of fairyland with all the lights are just what you see, if you're really tuned into it.'

There were all these bushes, just ordinary bushes,
but they had like fairy lights on them.
You'd come up to them and they'd go off,
then the lights would go on again.
It was like going into a disco. There were
so many lights, just white lights.
It was joyous, like a celebration.

LUCILLE

Writer and international teacher, Michael J Roads, has also visited the silvern realms, which he captures beautifully. 'Beyond the hill everything is shrouded in silver light; there is no distant vision. All is here and now,' he tells. 'The physical tree is clearly apparent, yet within and without are other dimensions of tree. Within is a similar flowing spreading stretch of rainbow light, permeated by countless numerous bee-sized beings of intense light. I cannot see any form to them, just light … and energy. But oh, what energy![41]

In these descriptions, you get a real taste of how the fairy dimensions look and feel, sensing the exquisitely fine energy there. This is a higher vibration of being, where love, light and life merge into divine oneness, into pure bliss. Perhaps this helps explain why fairies are said to be part of the angelic hierarchy, as they also occupy a space of light and love and perpetual bliss.

In this realm there is only here and now;
all else is shrouded in a silver nothingness.

MICHAEL J ROADS[42]

What's interesting about these and other accounts of the fairy realms is that none of the people concerned sought fairies initially. The fairies found them, introducing them to a world, a way of being, far beyond anything they could have imagined.

Michigan writer and engineer, Penny Kelly, had no interest or belief in fairies until she began to see them in the vineyard she tends with her husband. Over a number of years, the fairies reached out to Penny and taught her many things about herself and the intricacies of nature. Sometimes this wisdom came easily. Sometimes it came slowly and painfully. Frequently, she was aware of being stretched physically, mentally and spiritually.

Penny's life with the fairies began one day when she wandered up to the hill above the vineyard and crossed without warning into a golden world. 'The hill appeared like a golden, glowing mountain with miniature fields and clearings and tiny paths that criss-crossed in many directions. There were tall weeds and short trees grouped around small thatched doors,' she explains. 'Everything glowed as if lighted from within ... No matter which direction I looked, I saw the golden miniature world of the elves overlaid by a golden version of the reality I lived in.'[43]

Since then, Penny has entered the fairy realms on her farm on more than one occasion. 'This vineyard was the world of the elves,' she tells. 'Again there were the small trees, clearings, paths crossing here and there, leading to miniature doorways concealed in the tall grasses, hitching posts in yards ... and smoke arising from hidden chimneys.'[44]

As you read these accounts, more clues about the fairy kingdom emerge. You begin to sense our world is just one of many worlds within worlds. You also see that the fairy world isn't separate from us. It exists alongside, inside and around our own. It's interesting to note that when Bob, Lucille, Michael and Penny had their remarkable experiences, they remained in the same landscape. There were still the same trees and other natural landmarks present, but at the same time they were somewhere altogether different. They had each entered a subtler world than their everyday world. This new world had a different look, energy and hue. It was there that fairy creatures went about their work without impediment.

These amazing insights remind us that we do live alongside the fairies. They also show us that as well as there being numerous worlds within worlds, there's a vast array of fairy creatures going about their lives. Some people are lucky enough to cross over into one or more of the fairy worlds and to meet the fairies there. Sometimes the fairies step into our world and make contact. Regardless of the dynamic, know that wherever you are right now the fairies are less than the bat of an eyelid away, and that there's so much more to be discovered about fairies.

Entering Fairyland

The opportunity to glimpse or sense fairies is only one of the many profound experiences available to you, when you step inside the secret world of fairies. If you want to tread these enchanted ways, then take the road less travelled, as that's where life's true magic lies. In this space of infinite possibilities, the impossible becomes possible. It's a journey that can transform you, body and spirit. But before you set out, be sure your intentions are pure. Then if you really want to walk between worlds, leave behind everything that's familiar. Let go of all thoughts of who you are and what you've achieved. What you hold in your heart is all that matters.

> *Be sure you know what it is you seek,*
> *before you enter the realm of the fairy.*

Seeking out fairies is an exquisite journey, but not always an easy one, because it demands a great deal. It demands authenticity and courage—a willingness to step outside your comfort zone. This journey asks that you walk between worlds: between the everyday world you know well, and the exquisite worlds that lie beyond. To make headway, you need to be honest about yourself. About the bits you like, as well as the bits you don't like. You also need the courage to walk in places that are unfamiliar to you, and to change those parts of you that need changing.

To prepare yourself for the journey, it helps to work on lifting your life energy by connecting lovingly and profoundly with nature. Start to familiarise yourself with in-between places. Remember these gateways between worlds are not so much physical doors as invisible pathways beyond our world of form. These are paths of great power. They hold much promise but also many pitfalls. So be clear in your heart about what you seek. This is the time to work on your transparency, because once you enter the realms of the fairy everything is seen—your beauty, your potential, your fragility, your shadow self.

If you dare to set out on this path, sooner or later the fears that bind you will surface. Everything you thought you knew, believed in or wished for will be taken apart piece by piece, then weighed in the fire of truth. You may feel as if you're alone on the edge of the abyss and in some ways you are, because all you've clung to and hoped for has no relevance here. The only way forward is to face your fears. Allow them to become your friend. Once you acknowledge them, they will offer you a much larger, more powerful vision of yourself. They will set you free.

This is no easy process. It may take you to the limits of your endurance. But should you persevere, the journey will liberate you. There will be times when you may be tempted to abandon your fairy quest, to bury your pain and confusion. But having travelled this far, do not falter or draw back. Simply note the size and shape of each fear. Take time to see how this fear imprisons you. Stay focused on this fear. Note how it changes shape. Study it again in its new form. Notice how your fear shapeshifts in an attempt to avoid your gaze. Stay with it and see how it slowly fades, then dies. When you can face each fear as if surfaces, you get to see your fears as they really are. Shadows which haunt your every thought and action. Only in knowing your fears intimately can you be liberated from them, to then move more easily into the light-filled realms of the fairy.

Once you've conquered your fears, new choices beckon. The past and all it has brought you is behind you. The future is as yet unwritten. As you linger in this in-between space, you may doubt you have what it takes, but don't shrink back. In this moment, you have the chance to know yourself, to be free. Commit yourself to the journey and all it may teach you. Surrender your will to the divine underpinning of all creation and await its guidance.

The past and all it has brought you is behind you.
The future, as yet unwritten, stretches ahead of you.

With your fears dispersed and your compass set, things will shift. You'll find yourself bathed in a love beyond description. Suddenly, everything you ache for will be within reach. Here in the realm of the fairy, beyond time and space as you know it, you'll see for yourself how fluid life is. And how fluid your life can be. In this luminous space, as time bends and twists in on itself, you'll experience the great nothingness from which everything is formed.

In that exquisite moment, you finally arrive in the place of limitless potential. Your potential. It is time for you to taste your own fullness. To see with the eyes of spirit. You realise that in fact you were never alone. You were always part of something too vast and lovely, too powerful to name. As your soul dances to see life in all its beauty, the old you drops away. From this moment on, you're blessed to seek out and recognise the deep magic of life, wherever you find yourself.

Journey's End

When you enter fairyland with the right motives, you learn more about life than you ever thought possible. In time, you come home to your deepest soul yearnings. But your journey doesn't end there. Then it will be time to gather up all you've gained in the fairy realms, and bring it back with you to everyday life.

At first, your homecoming may be bittersweet. It certainly was for me. While my heart sang to be with those I loved, I was painfully aware of so many things I'd never noticed in everyday life before. The cruelty I now witnessed towards the living earth was at first unbearable. When I saw a tree cut down, or the earth gouged out, it felt as if I was being torn limb from limb. My world, which had once seemed so colourful, now seemed to have been painted in black and white.

If you come to these enchanted realms with the right motives, your dreams will indeed come true.

What I've since learnt is that this is no cause for despair. In truth, your enchanted journey has just begun. You'll now know without a shadow of a doubt that the fairy spirits of rocks and trees and plants are with you. They will help feed you body and spirit from day to day. As you go about your days, you'll begin to see what the fairies see: the fragility and utter preciousness of life. You may well find yourself able to speak with the plants and trees. To hear a message in the cry of a bird. To feel the earth's heartbeat beneath your feet. Your soul will sing with gratitude to experience such moments.

You may also be able to pick up on other people's thoughts and emotions. Alongside their love and kindness, you'll discern their envy and anger, their darkest desires. This may well sadden you, until you begin to understand the immense responsibility that a closer connection to life brings. In seeing life as it really is, your choice then is how to respond to the darker energies apparent to you.

As you dig deep, you find that place inside which inspires you to walk the path of harmlessness, beauty and wisdom. And because yours is now the tongue that cannot lie, there's no difficulty for you to be authentic in all you say and do, for you know that to do any less will shrivel your soul. Having tasted the absolute loveliness of life, you willingly shed your light in life's dark places. By rising above the pain and pettiness, you bathe everything and everyone you encounter in your radiance, often without realising it. Your presence alone gives others a real sense of safety and promise, amid life's confusion and despair.

Like the fairies you begin to live a world
that's ever-lovely and ever-becoming.

In the past, you were awake to the everyday world, but had no sense of your enchanted self. Now you live between worlds. You are still a creature of flesh and blood, but you also inhabit the rich world of spirit. Your loving connection to the fairy realms helps you discover more of your own immeasurable beauty and potential. As life opens up for you, you're in awe of the miracles that unfold daily. You begin to see the sheer loveliness of the earth, sky and stars, and to realise you're part of this beauty and always will be.

No aspect of nature is too small for your love and attention, as you now know from the depths of your being that every life matters. Your soul sings to know the rocks, plants and trees are your friends. That the earth's many creatures are your brothers and sisters. Now you willingly seek out wild places and nurture that part of you that remains forever wild and free until, like the fairies, you begin to live in a world that's ever-lovely and ever-becoming, brimful of life and hope.

As a tree gave its life so you could
glimpse the world of the fairies,
why not plant a small tree or a plant to
celebrate all you've discovered here?

Further Reading

Altman, Nathaniel, *The Deva Handbook: How to Work with Nature's Subtle Energies,* Destiny Books, Inner Traditions, Rochester, Vermont, 1995.

Charters, Daphne, *Forty Years with the Fairies,* R J Stewart Books, 2008.

Crombie, Robert Ogilvie, *Meeting Fairies: My Remarkable Encounters with Nature Spirits,* Allen And Unwin, Sydney, 2009.

Findhorn Community, The, *The Findhorn Garden: Pioneering a New Vision of Man and Nature in Cooperation,* Harper & Row, New York 1975.

Hawken, Paul, *The Magic Of Findhorn: The Extraordinary Community Where Man Co-Operates with Plants, Where People Are Transformed, Where Nothing Is Impossible and Legends Are Reborn,* Souvenir Press, London, 1975.

Helliwell, Tanis, *Summer with the Leprechauns: A True Story,* Blue Dolphin Publishing, Nevada City, 1997.

Hodson, Geoffrey, *Man's Supersensory and Spiritual Powers,* Theosophical Publishing House, Adyar, India, 1964.

Kelly, Penny, *The Elves Of Lily Hill Farm: A Partnership with Nature,* Lily Hill Publishing, Lawton, Michigan, 2005.

Maclean, Dorothy, *To Hear the Angels Sing: An Odyssey of Co-Creation with the Devic Kingdom,* Findhorn Publications, Forres, 1980.

Manouge, Vivienne, *Faeries of the Wild, Wild Moon*, Wellman Books, Chester, 2000.

Roads, Michael J, *Journey into Nature: A Spiritual Adventure*, H J Kramer Inc, California, 1990.

Stewart, R J, *The Living World of the Faery*, Mercury Publishing, Lake Toxaway, NC, 1995.

Todd, Lorna, *A Healer's Journey into the Light*, Bantam Books, London, 1995.

Von Holstein, Verena Stael, *Nature Spirits and What They Say*, Floris Books, Edinburgh, 2004.

Wright, Machaelle Small, *Perelandra Garden Workbook*, Perelandra Ltd, Jefferson, Virginia 1987.

References

1 C.S. Lewis, *The Lion, The Witch and The Wardrobe*, Geoffrey Bles Ltd, London, 1950

2 Rosemary Ellen Guiley, www.visionaryliving.com

3 Robert Ogilvie Crombie, *Meeting Fairies: My Remarkable Encounters with Nature Spirits*, Allen and Unwin, Sydney, 2009, p. 31

4 Robert Ogilvie Crombie, *Meeting Fairies: My Remarkable Encounters with Nature Spirits*, Allen and Unwin, Sydney, 2009, p. 31

5 Kim Del Rio, *Fairy Sighting*, http://paranormal.about.com/library/blstory_march03_15.htm March 2003

6 www.open-sesame.com/fairyencounters.html, chat session

7 www.realitywalker.com, chat session, 22 November 2009

8 Christopher Frayling, *Mad, Bad and Dangerous? The Scientist and The Cinema*, Reaktion Books, London, 2005

9 R J Stewart, *The Living World of the Faery*, Mercury Publishing, Lake Toxaway, North Carolina,1995, p. 13

10 Enid Blyton, *The Magic Faraway Tree*, Wyman and Sons, London,1943

11 Robert Ogilvie Crombie, *Meeting Fairies: My Remarkable Encounters with Nature Spirits*, Allen and Unwin, Sydney, 2009, pp. 2-8

12 R.J.Stewart, Fairy Congress Lecture, Skalitude, California, June 2010

13 Eugene O'Neill, *Long Day's Journey Into Night*, 1956

14 www.realitywalker.com, chat session, 12 April 2010

15 Dorothy Maclean, *To Hear the Angels Sing: An Odyssey of Co-Creation with the Devic Kingdom*, Findhorn Publications, Forres, 1980

16 Bruce A. Shuman, *Beyond The Library of the Future: More Alternatives For The Public Library*, Greenwood Publishing Group, Connecticut, 1997, p. 160

17 www.realitywalker.com, chat session, 12 April 2010

18 www.realitywalker.com/nature-spirits/fairy-tales-and-tales-of-fairies/comment-page-4/#comments

19 James M. Barrie, *Peter and Wendy*, Hodder & Stoughton, London 1911, Chapter 3

20 Arielle Ford, 'Damanhur: Italy's Utopian Eco Society', *Aspire Magazine*, February/ March 2008, www.aspiremag.net/damanhur-italys-utopian-eco-society

21 Verena Stael von Holstein, *Nature Spirits and What They Say*, Floris Books, Edinburgh, 2004, p. 15

22 Tanis Helliwell, *Summer With the Leprechauns: A True Story*, Blue Dolphin Publishing, Nevada City, 1997

23 Kat Harrison, *The Leaves of the Shepherdess*, Erocx1 Blog, 10 April 2008, http://erocx1.blogspot.com/2008/04/leaves-of-shepherdess-by-kat-harrison.html

24 Reb Andersen, *Warm Smiles from Cold Mountains: Dharma Talks on Zen Meditation*, Rodmell Press, Berkeley, 2005, p. 84

25 Denise Diamond, *The Complete Book of Flowers*, Theosophical Publishing House, London, 1990, p. 256

26 Denise Diamond, *The Complete Book of Flowers*, Theosophical Publishing House, London, 1990, p. 256

27 Catherine Morgan, *The Way of the Fairies: A Workbook for Healing the Earth and Ourselves*, Createspace, Charleston, 2009

28 Alberto Villoldo, *The Four Insights: Wisdom, Power and Grace of the Earthkeepers*, Hay House, New York, 2006, p. 68

29 www.realitywalker.com, chat session, 16 February, 2010

30 Robert Ogilvie Crombie, *Meeting Fairies: My Remarkable Encounters with Nature Spirits*, Allen and Unwin, Sydney, 2009, pp. 52-55

31 www.fairygardens.com/sightings/adult9.html

32 Penny Kelly, *The Elves of Lily Hill Farm: A Partnership with Nature*, Lily Hill Publishing, Lawton, Michigan, 2005, p. 34

33 Michael J Roads, *Journey Into Nature*, H J Kramer Inc, California, 1990, p. 160

34 Penny Kelly, *The Elves of Lily Hill Farm: A Partnership with Nature*, Lily Hill Publishing, Lawton, Michigan, 2005, p. 18

35 www.realitywalker.com, chat session, 12 April 2010
36 Jay Pettina, *The Whispering Goblin*, http://paranormal.about.com/
    library/weekly/aa021703c.htm
37 Vivienne Manouge, *Fairies of the Wild, Wild Moon*, Wellman Books,
    Nova Scotia, 2000, p. 44
38 Kat Morgenstern, 'Corn (Zea mays)', 'Indian Corn', 'Maize—History
    and Uses', *Sacred Earth*, www.sacredearth.com/ethnobotany/
    plantprofiles/corn.php, September 2007
39 Kat Morgenstern, 'Cacao (Theobroma)—History and Uses', *Sacred
    Earth*, www.sacredearth.com/ethnobotany/plantprofiles/cacao.php
40 Charles Kingsley, *Westward Ho!: Or the Voyages and Adventures of Sir
    Amyas Leigh, Knight, of Burrough, In The County of Devon, In The
    Reign of Her Most Glorious Majesty, Queen Elizabeth, Rendered Into
    Modern English by Charles Kingsley*, Cornell University Library
    Print, New York, 1878, p 266
41 Michael J Roads, *Journey Into Nature: A Spiritual Adventure*, H J
    Kramer Inc, California, 1990, p. 157
42 Michael J Roads, *Journey Into Nature: A Spiritual Adventure*, H J
    Kramer Inc, California, 1990, p. 158
43 Penny Kelly, *The Elves of Lily Hill Farm: A Partnership with Nature*,
    Lily Hill Publishing, Lawton, Michigan, 2005, p. 8
44 Penny Kelly, *The Elves of Lily Hill Farm: A Partnership with Nature*,
    Lily Hill Publishing, Lawton, Michigan, 2005, p. 16

Acknowledgements

Inside The Secret Life of Fairies was born decades ago, thanks to my parents Joan and Douglas, and my fearless Scottish grandmother Rose, and their strong connection had to the kingdom of the fairy. I'm also grateful to the wise generation of elders, who surrounded me as a child, unassuming yet remarkable souls with a lifetime of profound experiences with living nature, which they lovingly shared.

I am deeply indebted to the many individuals who entrusted me with their own precious, often healing encounters with fairies. Thanks too to such towering figures as Robert Ogilvie Crombie, Geoffrey Hodson, Dorothy Maclean, Eileen and Peter Caddy, who left us with countless stepping-stones to the kingdom of the fairy; to the world's great fairy illustrators long gone Arthur Rackham, Frances Hodgson Burnett and countless others, and to the many remarkable indigenous peoples across the planet who continue to honour and nurture the nature spirits in spite of so much personal hardship.

The book would not have happened without my wonderfully supportive publishing team at Hay House – Leon, Rosie, Errin and Rhett. Thanks too to Michelle, Elaine, Alexandra, Diane, Clemence, Rachel and Tom in London for their efforts. And endless gratitude to all my dear friends, who have journeyed with me over the years as the book was taking shape, who never doubted, but encouraged and supported me in dozens of loving ways.

Huge thanks to my dear Derek who never questions the journeys I take. He is without doubt the wind beneath my wings. And to the Great Spirit my soul gratitude for the precious gift of life and all the breath-taking possibilities you send my way.

About the Author

Maggie Hamilton is the author of a number of spiritual and social justice books, which have been published in Australia, New Zealand, Holland, Italy, China, Lithuania, Korea, the Arab States and Brazil. Her travels have taken her to deserts and sacred mountains, to temples and cathedrals, labyrinths and standing-stones, where each time a new face of the sacred has revealed itself. After many years in book publishing, Maggie now devotes her time to sacred journeying, writing, teaching and mentoring, and to her own practice – www.maggiehamilton.org and www. secretlifeoffairies@wordpress.com

If you have fairy thoughts or encounters you'd like to share, email Maggie on contact@maggiehamilton.org

We hope you enjoyed this Hay House book. If you'd like to receive our online catalogue featuring additional information on Hay House books and products, or if you'd like to find out more about the Hay Foundation, please contact:

Hay House Australia Pty. Ltd.,
P.O. Box 7201, Alexandria, NSW 2015
Phone: +61 2 9669 4299
www.hayhouse.com.au

Published in the USA by:
Hay House, Inc., P.O. Box 5100, Carlsbad, CA 92018-5100
Phone: (760) 431-7695 • *Fax:* (760) 431-6948
www.hayhouse.com®

Published in the United Kingdom by:
Hay House UK, Ltd., The Sixth Floor, Watson House,
54 Baker Street, London, W1U 7BU
Phone: 020 3927 7290
www.hayhouse.co.uk

Published in India by:
Hay House Publishers India, Muskaan Complex, Plot No. 3, B-2,
Vasant Kunj, New Delhi, 110 070
Phone: 91-11-4176-1620 • *Fax:* 91-11-4176-1630
www.hayhouse.co.in

Access New Knowledge.
Anytime. Anywhere.

Learn and evolve at your own pace
with the world's leading experts.

www.hayhouseU.com

Printed in the United States
By Bookmasters